An Archaeological Study of the Bayeux Tapestry

An Archaeological Study of the Bayeux Tapestry

The Landscapes, Buildings and Places

Trevor Rowley

PEN & SWORD ARCHAEOLOGY

First published in Great Britain in 2016 by
Pen & Sword Archaeology
an imprint of
Pen & Sword Books Ltd
47 Church Street
Barnsley
South Yorkshire
S70 2AS

ISBN 978 1 78159 380 6

A CIP catalogue record for this book is available from the British Library

Typeset in Ehrhardt by
Mac Style Ltd, Bridlington, East Yorkshire
Printed and bound by CPI Group (UK) Ltd, Croydon, CR0 4YY

Pen & Sword Books Ltd incorporates the imprints of Pen & Sword
Archaeology, Atlas, Aviation, Battleground, Discovery, Family History,
History, Maritime, Military, Naval, Politics, Railways, Select, Transport,
True Crime, and Fiction, Frontline Books, Leo Cooper, Praetorian Press,
Seaforth Publishing and Wharncliffe.

For a complete list of Pen & Sword titles please contact
PEN & SWORD BOOKS LIMITED
47 Church Street, Barnsley, South Yorkshire, S70 2AS, England
E-mail: enquiries@pen-and-sword.co.uk
Website: www.pen-and-sword.co.uk

Contents

Acknowledgements

I would like to thank all those people who have encouraged me in the writing of this book and have helped with information, ideas, typing, translation, editing, and cartography. Notably Martin Biddle, Linda Kent, Martin Henig, Maggie Kneen, Sylvie Lemangen, Michael Lewis, Gale Owen-Crocker, Jane Rowley and Richard Rowley. Needless to say any mistakes, omissions or misinterpretations belong to me alone.

I would also like to thank the city and people of Bayeux for permission to include the many reproductions from the Bayeux Tapestry.

This book is dedicated to my lovely wife, Jane.

Foreword

In writing this book I have had the opportunity of combining two lifelong academic passions - the Normans and landscape history. I have interpreted 'archaeology' in the title very broadly to include the historic landscape of the mid-eleventh century in England and North-western France. Some may be disappointed at the meagre representation of artifactual analysis, but I would point them towards the fine work of Michael Lewis and David Wilson amongst others. This book, I believe, represents one of the first attempts to explore the landscape setting in which the events depicted on the Bayeux Tapestry took place. For the most part the Tapestry provides topographic detail grudgingly, but it does give many pointers, which used with other sources helps us understand more fully the geography of Normandy and England in 1066.

As I have been writing a *leitmotif* has emerged in the form of the re-occurring importance of the classical legacy; both in the events surrounding 1066 and in the Tapestry itself. In the eleventh century a great deal more Roman masonry and carving would have been visible in northern Europe than is the case today and its influence on the Norman world seems to have been profound. The Norman rebuilding of England in the neo-classical Romanesque style was itself a form of colonialism reminiscent of Roman Britain. Also it has been recognized for some time that the design of many of the buildings on the Tapestry is based on contemporary illuminated manuscripts, whose origins date back to the Roman era. More recently surviving Roman figurative carving, such as that on Trajan's Column in Rome, has been identified as an important source for some of the Tapestry's choreography. The Norman Conquest would have been played out in a landscape where Roman antiquities would have been a common sight. On the Tapestry only Pevensey is identified as a place where there was a surviving Roman fortress, but it is probable that Roman fortifications would also have been used at Dover, Rochester and elsewhere. Moreover, both armies would have used the decaying Roman road system wherever possible in England and in Normandy. As William the Conqueror consolidated his hold on England after the Battle of Hastings echoes of the Roman conquest of Britain a thousand years earlier seem to have both materially helped and inspired him.

Trevor Rowley
Appleton, June 1 2016

Introduction

The Bayeux Tapestry is the greatest surviving historical chronicle from the Anglo-Norman era. 'As a large-scale picture of warfare' at the close of the Anglo-Saxon era 'it stands alone', observed Frank Stenton, the doyen of Anglo-Saxon historians. 'But its ultimate distinction lies ... in the artist's grasp of his theme, his skilful arrangement of contrasted scenes, his mastery of the technique of composition, and above all, the curious air of vitality ... that runs through the whole long work.'[1] The Bayeux Tapestry depicts a specific version of the Battle of Hastings in 1066 and the events leading up to it. Many of the principal characters involved in the conflict are shown and the Tapestry portrays Saxons and Normans of various ranks, secular and ecclesiastical, engaged in a range of military, political and ceremonial activities.

Over the years the Bayeux Tapestry has been the object of intense speculation. Its contents have been analysed from every conceivable point of view. When was it embroidered, where was it made, who was responsible for its production and how should its images and narrative be interpreted? These and many other questions have been directed towards the hanging, but it is an artefact which is rich in ambiguity at every level. Part of the joy of the Tapestry is that although it ostensibly tells the straightforward story of William the Conqueror's successful invasion of England, on deeper examination it turns out to be anything but straightforward.

There is probably more of a consensus about when it was executed than any other aspect of its interpretation. Most scholars now believe that it was made within two decades of 1066, but at that point concord ends. There is a general agreement that the Tapestry was produced in England, probably at Canterbury, but some historians believe that it was created elsewhere in England or in France. William the Conqueror's half brother Bishop Odo of Bayeux remains the leading contender for having sponsored the Tapestry, but there are many other candidates, both English and French. Recently it has been suggested that the Tapestry was not the responsibility of one individual at all, but a corporate production by the monks of St Augustine's, Canterbury.[2] Furthermore, it has been argued that the real subject of the Tapestry was not the triumph of Duke William, but the punishment of the English, and that it was a sophisticated parable. Its function was to illustrate the punishment meted out to the English by God for Harold's perjury and the accumulated sins of the English people.[3]

Traditionally, the story of the conquest of England as depicted by the Tapestry has been interpreted as Norman propaganda, largely following the narrative set out by the contemporary Norman chroniclers William of Poitiers (c.1020–90) and William of Jumièges (c.1000–1070). The Tapestry does appear to justify the Norman invasion, but it also acknowledges the valour of King Harold and the English defenders. Some scholars have suggested that the Tapestry is not a piece of Norman propaganda at all, but if analysed closely presents a balanced representation of events; others have gone further and claim that it carries a subversive English message. In reality, the Tapestry is capable of being interpreted in many ways and most scenes are ambiguous in some aspect of their meaning. For example, 'Was it made so that Normans could impress the subjugated foe? Or so that the English could flatter, yet secretly insult the victors?'[4]

The Tapestry has long been recognized as an important source of information for archaeologists and architectural historians, portraying ships, weaponry, clothing, castles, churches and a wide range of other buildings and artefacts. Many scholars have uncritically accepted that the Tapestry depicts authentic eleventh-century buildings and artefacts and Grape is typical in claiming that the Tapestry was 'a record of first hand observation'.[5] Brown went even further to pronounce that the Tapestry's images 'offer us an archaeological encyclopaedia'[6] while Maclagan had earlier claimed that the Tapestry provides 'our best authority for the arms and armour of the period'.[7] There had been some dissenting voices that had queried the reliability of the Tapestry evidence and as far back as 1894 Archer had questioned its artefactual authority on the grounds of 'its curious and in some cases more than curious archaeology'.[8] In his canonical work Wilson where possible compared the images on the Tapestry against the available archaeological evidence, and he observed that 'a great deal of what is seen in the hanging is ... formulaic and cannot be said to do more than indicate the object illustrated'.[9] New ground was broken when Brooks and Walker argued that the Tapestry must be used with considerable reserve as an authority on matters of warfare and history and especially the manner of King Harold's death at Hastings. They also drew attention to similarities in the Tapestry's images to those found in contemporary manuscripts from Canterbury and on Trajan's Column in Rome.[10]

Some recent studies have been even more sceptical of the traditional interpretation of the Tapestry images at their face value. Lewis and Owen-Crocker, in particular, have reassessed the accuracy of the Tapestry to determine how reliable an image of the eleventh-century world it presents. They have critically analysed the depiction of buildings, arms, ships, dress and other elements and traced their original pictorial sources, largely from the manuscripts which would have been available to the Tapestry's creators. Their conclusion is that much of the imagery is the product of the art historical tradition of the period, and that little of what is portrayed should be taken literally. Furthermore, they have identified many examples of iconography taken from manuscripts that were in the library of St Augustine's Abbey in Canterbury at the time the Tapestry was made.[11]

Despite the considerable volume of revisionist assessment published since the Tapestry was moved to its present home in the Musée de la Tapisserie de Bayeux,[12] one dimension of the work has not received the attention it perhaps deserves – the examination of the landscape of England and France against which the story of the Norman Conquest is played out. An important aspect of the Tapestry story is that it presents a continuous historical narrative of events within a recognized time frame. Furthermore, these events take place against an identifiable geography of England and France. The main purpose of this book is to try and understand some aspects of the historical geography in which the Tapestry is placed. Where did the momentous events portrayed actually take place and how much can the hanging tell us about the landscape of mid-eleventh-century France and England?

The events on the Tapestry alternate between England and France, divided by sea crossings, but although a few places are actually named there is surprisingly little detailed information about precise locations. The geography of the Bayeux Tapestry, like its historical narrative, is opaque. The Tapestry does feature real places, but were these actually where the events took place? Another layer of uncertainty is added by doubts about whether some of the events took place at all, or at least in the form they appear on the Tapestry.

The story as told on the Tapestry starts in England and then after a Channel crossing moves to Ponthieu, a feudal county to the north of Normandy. There follow a number of scenes set in unspecified places in Normandy, after which the action moves to Brittany. A military campaign is fought in the Breton Marches and then the location moves to Bayeux back in Normandy. The sea crossing back to England is followed by a series of largely ceremonial scenes set in Westminster. Following another Channel crossing the action reverts to France, where the invasion fleet is being prepared and an army is raised. Following the embarkation and crossing of the invasion fleet to Pevensey, the Norman forces move to Hastings and a series of pre-battle events take place, presumably in the vicinity of Hastings. Finally the battle is fought at an unnamed location.

Only ten places are named on the Tapestry. Four are in England – Bosham, Pevensey and Hastings; Westminster is also identified through the naming of the church of St Peter the Apostle. There are six named places in France – Belrem (Beaurain) in Ponthieu, Mont-St-Michel on the border of Normandy and Brittany, and Dol, Rennes and Dinan in Brittany, with Bayeux as the only Norman location that is recorded. The only named topographical feature in the whole of the Tapestry (apart from Mont-St-Michel) is the River Cousenon, which formed the boundary between Brittany and Normandy.

This means that there are some notable geographical omissions, principally, the Norman capital of Rouen, which is clearly depicted, but not named. It might also have been expected that several other important locations in the duchy, such as

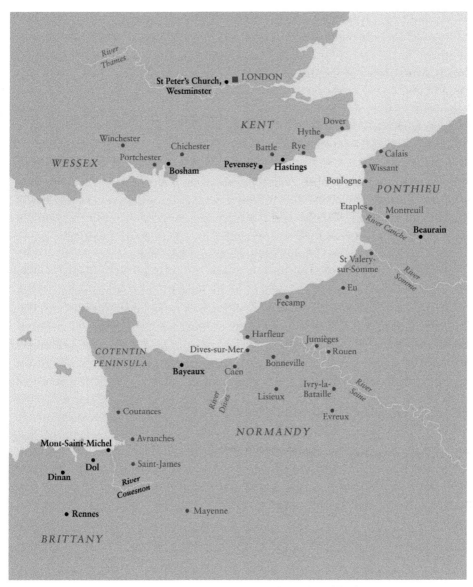

Plan showing places named on the Bayeux Tapestry and mentioned in the text.

Caen, Fécamp and Dives sur Mer, where the invasion fleet was mustered, would have been identified. It is clear that the Tapestry is therefore no more a detailed geographical itinerary than it is an accurate historical chronicle. The designer was intent on telling a particular story in a particular way, where geographical features and accurate historical details were not essential. Nonetheless, the geographical balance that emerges is still surprising. Out of the six French places named only one, Bayeux, is actually in Normandy; two if Mont-St-Michel is included, a site which could equally be attributed to Brittany. There are no places named in Upper Normandy, the heartland and the seat of the Norman dukes. In this omission as in others the Tapestry is at odds with the chroniclers on whom we rely for many details of the story of conquest. William of Poitiers, William of Jumièges and Orderic Vitalis (1075–*c*.1142) all describe important events taking place in Upper Normandy in the run-up to the invasion.[13] It is also striking that about 70 per cent of the French coverage in the Tapestry takes place outside of Normandy, some of it based in the relatively small county of Ponthieu and the remainder in the Duchy of Brittany.

There are justifiable doubts about the accuracy of both the Ponthieu and Breton episodes and the manner in which they are portrayed on the Tapestry. Stories of such events, unrelated to the invasion, may have been in circulation at the time that the Tapestry was composed and were included in order to make a particular point, perhaps to emphasize Earl Harold's obligation to Duke William.

On occasion the Tapestry does attempt to portray a landscape, albeit impressionistically. These episodes tend to be linked to events involving intense activity and rely to some extent on the portrayal of rapid or dramatic movement. Indeed, much of the Tapestry depends upon movement in the form of journeys, processions and battles. Some of the most graphic scenes involve men and horses and manage to create a sense of a real world, despite the absence of specific topographic features. These are notably the journey to Bosham; the arrest of Harold and negotiations for his release; the Breton campaign and Harold's oath; the death of Edward and Harold's coronation; the preparation for the invasion and the fleet sailing for England; the preamble to the battle and the battle itself. It is one of the many great strengths of the Tapestry that it is able to create a sense of place with minimum pictorial assistance. The detailed analysis of the individual parts should not diminish the immense impact of the whole.

Chapter 1

The Bayeux Tapestry

The pictorial representation of great historical events has a long pedigree extending back into prehistory. Roman and Carolingian rulers recorded their victories as historical narratives in stone, wall paintings and textile hangings which decorated their halls and palaces. The use of illustrated narrative strips was popular in early medieval Scandinavia and Germany. Examples are to be found on the eighth-century Franks Casket, believed to be of Northumbrian origin, now in the British Museum, made of carved whalebone, and on the remains of a wall-hanging found in the ninth-century Oseberg ship burial in Norway. There are references to tapestries in twelfth-century French epic poetry, for instance, in the *Chanson de Girart de Roussillon*, in which the guest chamber of a count's palace was 'everywhere spread with tapestries and hangings'. Chroniclers record that after William the Conqueror's death, servants ran off with hangings from his palace in Rouen.[1] Hangings had been authorized, even encouraged, by the Council of Arras in 1025 as one of the means of edifying and informing the

Rear panel of the Franks Casket (British Museum). Eighth-century Anglo-Saxon whale's bone chest depicting the Taking of Jerusalem during the First Jewish-Roman War. In the upper-left section the Romans led by Titus attack the domed Temple of Jerusalem, while in the upper right the Jewish population flees. The inscription is partly in Old English and partly in Latin, some of the Latin has been transcribed phonetically into runic letters.

Christian faithful.[2] Even the depiction of military scenes was seen as suitable for display in places of worship, as demonstrated by a reference in the *Liber Eliensis*, compiled in the mid-twelfth century. Aelfleada, the wife of an English chieftain killed by Danes at the Battle of Maldon (AD 991), gave Ely church her husband's 'demesne lands and a necklace of gold and a coloured woven wall-hanging showing his deeds, in memory of his greatness'. There would therefore seem to have been no objection to the illustration of the fighting at Hastings, which had ostensibly been sanctioned by the pope. Pope Alexander II had endorsed William's cause by conferring a papal banner upon him 'as a sign of St Peter's approval, by which he might more safely and confidently attack the enemy'.[3]

Nevertheless such early surviving narrative tapestries are rare in Western Europe. There is an intriguing reference to a near-contemporary hanging to the Bayeux Tapestry in the work of Baudri de Bourgueil (d.1130). Baudri had been abbot of Borgueil in the Loire Valley from 1078 to 1107, when he became bishop of Dol. Baudri wrote a poem (dated 1099–1102) called the *Adelae Comitissae*, which was addressed to Adela, Countess of Blois and daughter of William the Conqueror. Writing in verse form he described a hanging in Adela's chamber, which told the story of William's conquest of England, starting with the appearance of Halley's Comet early in 1066 and finishing with the conquest of Kent. The author tells us that the hanging had captions and depicted the construction of the fleet and the

An eighteenth century painting of Bishop Odo, probable sponsor of the Bayeux Tapestry. (*Baron Gérard Museum, Bayeux*)

subsequent Channel crossing. On the face of it, this looks like a description of the Bayeux Tapestry located at Blois, in the Loire Valley, in the late eleventh century.[4] It is, however, unlikely that Baudri ever met Adele or saw her chamber, as elsewhere he admits the fictional quality of his poetry, 'but it's not true, I make it all up'. Nevertheless, his account mirrors the Tapestry to such a degree in some details that it is fair to assume he had actually seen it.[5] One scholar has recently argued that the Tapestry was actually produced in the Loire Valley at the monastery of Saint-Florent of Saumur. He proposes that the work was commissioned by King William as propaganda and managed by William, the abbot of St Florent, who was grateful to the king for coming to his father, Rivallon 1 of Dol's assistance in 1064. It is suggested that this would help explain the inclusion of the detailed coverage of the 'Breton Campaign'.[6]

It is generally, although not universally, accepted that the Bayeux Tapestry was sponsored by William the Conqueror's half-brother Bishop Odo of Bayeux (c.1035–97) and completed in time for the consecration of the new cathedral in Bayeux in 1077.[7] Odo was not only William's half-brother, he also played an important political role in Normandy in the years before the Conquest. He had been bishop of Bayeux from c.1050, and as such was second only to the archbishop of Rouen in clerical status in the duchy. Until the early 1080s he was a close ally of his brother William and undoubtedly performed a pivotal political role in the events leading up to the invasion of England. He would have been familiar with the geography of the Seine Valley and Lower Normandy and parts of Upper

The cedar chest in which the Bayeux Tapestry was kept in Bayeux Cathedral for several centuries.

Normandy as well. The bishop sailed with the invasion fleet and was at the Battle of Hastings. As such he would have been intimately acquainted both with the events of the Conquest and with the geographical framework in which they occurred. He was singularly well qualified to oversee the production of this masterpiece.

Apart from the sympathetic manner in which the bishop is portrayed in the Tapestry, perhaps the most powerful argument for Odo's role in creating the work was the nature of his own ambitious personality. Odo was an energetic and successful patron of the arts. The development of Bayeux as an intellectual centre and the conquest of England made him the second richest and second most powerful man in the Anglo-Norman world, with the capacity to call upon the artistic resources of the newly won kingdom. It is totally in keeping with Odo's character that he should commission a work which told graphically the story of how those riches were acquired, and at the same time giving himself a pivotal role in the representation of that achievement. It is possible that Odo commissioned the Tapestry to be completed in time for the consecration of his new cathedral in Bayeux on 14 July 1077. However, there is no general agreement about where it was intended to be hung. A recent suggestion is that it was intended for the great hall of Odo's lodge in Trenley Park outside Canterbury.[8]

In 1982–3 the Tapestry was cleaned and conserved before being moved to its new home in the Musée de la Tapisserie de Bayeux, a former seminary which was adapted to house the textile in an environmentally controlled unit.

This move allowed a detailed examination of the embroidery, including the back, to be carried out. This analysis stimulated a considerable amount of revisionary speculation about its origins, content and execution. In particular, a debate has raged about the Tapestry's sponsor. While the consensus is still that

General view of the tapestry as it is currently displayed in the Museum of the Tapestry, Bayeux where it has been housed since 1983.

Odo was involved in some way with its creation, several other candidates have been proposed. These include Queen Edith of Wessex, Edward the Confessor's wife (1025–75); Eustace II, Count of Boulogne (c.1020–87); Bishop Odo's vassals Wadard and Vital; the Loire Valley abbey of Saint-Florent of Saumur and even the disgraced Archbishop of Canterbury, Stigand (d.1072). Recently, an idea popular in the nineteenth century, that Queen Matilda was responsible for the tapestry, has been revived. A more credible suggestion is that Edith of Wessex was closely involved in making the Tapestry. She was both Harold's sister and widow of Edward the Confessor, placing her close to the centre of events in 1066. She is one of only three women depicted on the Tapestry, where she is seen weeping at the foot of Edward's deathbed. After the Conquest she moved into Wilton nunnery, a Benedictine convent near Salisbury, but appears to have established cordial relations with King William and continued to be one of the most influential English aristocrats until her death in 1075, when the *Anglo-Saxon Chronicle* records that 'The king had her brought to Westminster with great honour'. She is known to have been an accomplished needle worker and she ran a royal embroidery workshop, producing textiles for churches as well as Edward's robes of state. She was in a favourable position to have sponsored the politically balanced Tapestry, as interpreted by some scholars, but as with all the candidates there remain, and will remain, many unanswered questions about Edith's possible involvement in the production of the Bayeux Tapestry.[9]

A recent powerful reassessment of the Tapestry has argued that there was no external patron at all. Pastan and White believe that the Tapestry was the corporate work of the monks of St Augustine's, Canterbury, and was intended to be displayed in their abbey: 'The new abbey church had both the grandeur of conception and the physical amplitude for hanging the Bayeux Embroidery.'[10] Furthermore, it is suggested that its display in such a location would cater for a sophisticated audience, including the monks, who would have had the knowledge to interpret the hanging in all its complexity.

Despite its name the hanging is not technically a tapestry, but an embroidery of coloured wools on a linen background, consisting of eight separate panels joined together. It is 50cm wide and is now just under 70m long; the final section, having been partly destroyed, is much shorter than the others. The central part of the Tapestry depicts the story of the Conquest; at the top and bottom are narrow borders which are basically decorative, but occasionally complement the main narrative register. In scenes of heightened tension, the central story spreads out into the borders. The border decoration consists of birds, beasts and fish, many of them mythical in character, as well as scenes from fables and portraits of agriculture and hunting. There are also nude figures and others of a ribald nature that apparently comment on events in the main story. Some features, such as the moustaches shown on most of the English figures in the first part of the Tapestry and the shaven backs of heads of the Normans, are probably based on authentic

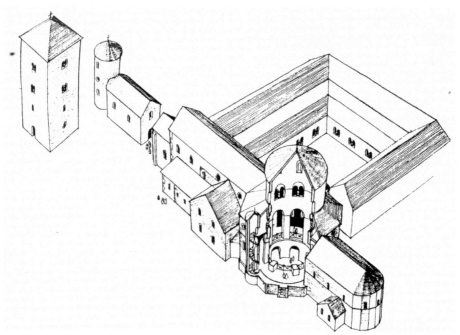

St Augustine's Abbey, Canterbury, reconstruction of the intended scheme in the mid–eleventh century. (*Urmston, P. Historic England*)

Ruins of St Augustine's Abbey church, Canterbury with Christ Church Cathedral in the background. It seems probable that this is where the Tapestry was made. The abbey's extensive library provided the material for many of the images.

characteristics, but are exaggerated to provide a convenient visual grammar to aid identification.

Eight colours are used in the Bayeux Tapestry: terracotta red, three different shades of green, two shades of blue and two of yellow. The colours are not used naturalistically; thus, horses are blue or buff, with legs and hooves portrayed in different and arbitrary colours. The use of unreal colouring gives an element of caricature which, together with lively outlines, is articulated with great skill. The effect of such different colours is not incongruous, as it is the tonal contrast rather than the degree of realism in the shades which makes the impact.[11]

Despite such variety, there is a remarkably uniform design throughout and because of this consistency it is generally believed to have been devised by a single artist working to the instructions of a patron, such as Bishop Odo. The designer was familiar with and used examples from illuminated manuscripts, sculpture, frescoes and oral sources. The visual flow of the narrative is controlled with trees and buildings used as punctuation. There are historical mistakes on the Tapestry which suggest that the artist/designer was not fully aware of the history, but was working from instructions, information and possibly some written phrases provided by his patron/sponsor, which he then incorporated into the Tapestry design.[12]

No evidence of an outline drawing or cartoon which was transferred on to the linen base has been found, although there must have been one originally. According to the eleventh-century *Life of St Dunstan* (d.988), as a young cleric Dunstan was asked to draw up designs for a young noblewoman to embroider on a stole. St Dunstan is associated with another story concerning textiles, when he comes upon a sick woman from London, who after following instructions to decorate her tunic 'with golden embroidery' is instantly healed.[13] The Anglo-Saxon embroidery style was combined split stitch and couching with silk and gold work or silver gilt thread. This style later flowered and became known as *Opus Anglicanum* (English work).

Hairstyles on the Bayeux Tapestry. The English, on the left were conventionally shown with long hair and moustaches, on the right the French were depicted with half shaven heads, while in the centre clerics were given a tonsure.

There are fifty-eight captions above the main part of the Tapestry; these consist largely of brief notes pointing out the names of some people and places. The captions are in abbreviated Latin and were possibly added after the pictorial narrative had been completed. Several words which appear on the Tapestry suggest an English origin, for example, *Ædwardus* rather than *Edwardus*, *ceastra* rather than *castra* and *Franci* rather than *Normani*. It has also been suggested that *Bagias* is an English hybridisation of the place-name Bayeux.

The Tapestry tells a unique version of events between 1064 and 1066, culminating in the victory of Duke William of Normandy over King Harold of England on 14 October 1066. It portrays events largely from a Norman viewpoint, starting with Harold's journey to France in 1064 or 1065. The purpose of this journey is not explained, but the Normans argued that Harold travelled as an emissary of King Edward in order to confirm Duke William's right to the English throne in the event of the Confessor's death without children. A sequence of events followed which tied Harold to William as his vassal, culminating in the swearing of a sacred oath in which Harold appears to pledge his loyalty to William. Almost immediately on his return to England the old king dies and Harold takes the throne. In response William raises an army and builds a fleet of ships for the invasion of England. The duke's fleet sails for England and after spending some time on the south coast the Norman and English armies engage at the Battle of Hastings and William is victorious. The Tapestry's version of the story omits much contemporary detail and ignores some important events, notably, Harold's journey to the north of England and victory over a Scandinavian army at Stamford Bridge on the eve of the Norman invasion in September 1066.

Several authorities argue that the original hanging was probably about 1.5m longer than its present 70m and portrayed William's triumphal entry into London and his coronation held on Christmas Day 1066. For centuries the Tapestry was folded and stored in a chest in Bayeux Cathedral, apart from eight days following the feast of St John the Baptist when it was displayed around the nave of the church. The uppermost part of the folded Tapestry would, therefore, have been the last panel, which would have been the most vulnerable to damp and decay. The survival of the majority of the Tapestry in such a well-preserved condition resulted from the fact that it was folded and thus protected for most of the time, being brought out of its box for only these eight days. Attention has also been drawn to the composition of the chest in Bayeux Cathedral where the Tapestry was housed for many centuries. The chest is large enough to have contained the Tapestry before it was lined in the eighteenth or nineteenth century and it has been argued that the Tapestry could have been protected by the preserving properties of the box itself. The chest appears to be made of cedar and, if so, the Tapestry spent the first 600 years or so of its life carefully folded into a chest impregnated with cedar oil, a natural moth repellent.[14]

The Tapestry is in the form of a long, thin strip with a visual momentum which ensures that the viewer moves onwards following a controlled, progressive

The west front of Bayeux Cathedral. Little of Bishop Odo's building, which was consecrated in 1077, survives on the exterior, although the later ground plan with its two western towers replicated Odo's church.

narrative. The Tapestry features around fifty scenes and, as the eye moves along the strip, so it advances through time through a sequence of images. In a world where literacy was restricted largely to the clergy, visual imagery was of great importance in the telling of stories and history. The use of hands, facial expressions and body language are vital to the telling of the story and contribute to the appeal of the Tapestry in surviving as a much admired artefact over 900 years after it was produced.

One of the most important characteristics of the Tapestry is that it is a picture cycle narrating a recent historical event; as such it conveys a naturalism missing from most contemporary art of that time. The sense of an evolving narrative is emphasized by the smooth transition from one scene to the next. In most eleventh-century art, such a progression is implied. This development gives the impression that the designer was acquainted with the details provided. Some of the anecdotal detail implies that the designer may have observed some of these events himself; for example, in the scene depicting the building of Hastings Castle, two men are shown fighting or 'play-fighting' with spades.[15] However, it has also been suggested that this scene reflects a misreading of a copy of a very similar scene on Trajan's Column in Rome, where soldiers are shown building a fort.[16]

Trajan's Column, Rome

Many of the images in the Tapestry are derived from classical sources, mostly from copies of illuminated manuscripts in circulation in the eleventh century. Trajan's Column in Rome is another possible source for imagery on the Tapestry. The column is a 42m (138ft) marble pillar erected in Trajan's Forum in AD 113 to commemorate Emperor Trajan's two wars against the Dacians. The monument bears carved accounts of Roman military victories, arranged in spiral strips round the cylindrical pillar, running from left to right, bottom to top.

Similarities between this triumphal monument and the Bayeux Tapestry have been noted since the eighteenth century. Recently, these parallels have been analysed in more detail.[17] Both Trajan's Column and the Tapestry consist of a continuous frieze depicting recent events in the form of long, narrow pictorial registers. The narrative is divided into discrete 'scenes', bounded by trees and buildings. Originally, the marble frieze sculptures on the Column would have been coloured and its resemblance to the Tapestry would have been even greater in the eleventh century.

Bishop Odo, the probable patron of the Tapestry, is known to have had a mansion in Rome and may well have visited the city. Another possible patron, Scolland, the abbot of St Augustine's, Canterbury, between 1070 and 1089, appears to have visited Rome in 1071–72 and could have been inspired by the column. Scolland came to Canterbury from Mont-St-Michel, a notable centre of manuscript production, and was himself an accomplished scribe.

Trajan's Column, Rome, showing soldiers building a fort during the Dacian Wars. The column was completed in AD 113.

The building of Hastings Castle on the Bayeux Tapestry, this scene may show men mock fighting with spades, or it may represent a misreading of a similar image on Trajan's column.

Illuminated manuscripts do provide details which can be compared to those on the Tapestry, but nowhere is there a comparable running historical narrative. Contemporary accounts of the events are contained in the written chronicles of the Normans and the English. For the most part the geographical setting is only of incidental importance and for the most part absent from these accounts. It is true that the Tapestry mostly ignores the physical setting of the story, but because it is a visual account it is obliged to provide some detail of place, the value of which is attested in the numerous extracts taken from the Tapestry to illustrate aspects of eleventh-century artefacts, culture and buildings.

Although there are relatively few specific, identifiable topographical illustrations, such as Mont-St-Michel, the River Cousenon and the site of the Battle of Hastings, the Tapestry does contain information about buildings and place. It names specific buildings and structures, such as Bosham Church, Hastings Castle and the Breton castles. Other named places include Beaurain (Nord) and Pevensey (Sussex) and in several scenes it is possible to identify the location from other indicators.

The People

The cast of the Tapestry includes a wide range of characters, from the king of England through to a dwarf-ostler. High- and low-ranking clerics are shown as well as rulers, nobles, servants and peasants. There are craftsmen, sailors, cavalrymen and archers. In all there are 626 human figures, added to which there are 190 horses, 35 dogs, 506 birds and other animals, including a wide range of mythological and fabled beasts.

Some attempt is made to distinguish the Normans from the English through dress, and many of the English soldiers, as well as Earl Harold, are portrayed wearing moustaches, while many of the Normans appear to have the backs of their heads shaven. Originally, this fashion appears to have derived from the Frankish custom of cropping the back of the head after defeat.

The Normans on the Tapestry are often depicted wearing tunics with divided skirts, otherwise known as culottes. Harold also wears them on horseback, both during and after his visit to Normandy, but generally they do not appear on English figures. Another distinguishing feature is that the Normans wear a range of garters, while the English normally appear without leg bands.

The conventional view of the Tapestry as an accurate record of mid-eleventh-century images has been challenged in recent years. It has been argued that many of the Tapestry's illustrations are based on scenes and motifs depicted in extant artwork, most notably, the illuminated manuscripts found in the Canterbury monastic schools.[18] Furthermore, it has been claimed that the depictions of buildings, clothes and objects in the Tapestry cannot be used as historical evidence for what was happening at the time of the Norman Conquest, as the designer was using illustrations that had been created over the previous two centuries.

God appearing to Abraham in front of a classical building with a portal and dome; features found on several buildings on the Tapestry. From the *Old English Illustrated Hexateuch. (BL. Cotton MS Claudius B. iv, fol. 37rs)*

While it is true that many of the images have their origins in other sources, the sum of the Tapestry is greater than its parts. We can see, for instance, that the image of one of the carpenters planing a plank probably has its origins in a similar representation from the Old English Hexateuch (the first six books of the Old Testament), but it has been significantly altered to meet the storyline of the Tapestry. Indeed, the image from the manuscript has been used as a source for two separate events on the Tapestry.[19]

The Landscape

For the most part, little attempt is made to illustrate details of the landscape in which the events on the Tapestry take place. Howe makes the point that we do not really know how the Anglo-Saxons viewed their landscape, but that their understanding of places was deeply shaped by textual representations, and he noted that 'the Anglo-Saxon tradition of cartography was far more narrative than visual'. He goes on to quote as an example the Old English poem *Maxims II*, 'cities may be seen from afar, those that are on the earth, the skilled work of giants, the artfully crafted work of wall-stones'.[20] Howe also argues that much of what we know about the Anglo-Saxon landscape we learn from land charters, which do not describe landscape features so much as the edges or boundaries of those features. When he writes, 'In the charters, landscape is not a vista to be contemplated but a sequence of signs to be walked',[21] he could equally be describing the landscapes of the Bayeux Tapestry. Hoskins observed, perhaps rather unfairly, that the Anglo-Saxons had 'no eye for scenery, any more than other hard-working farmers of later centuries'.[22] The creators of the Tapestry were not farmers; they were probably scholars and clerics with a keen eye for detail, including the landscape they inhabited. Their depiction of that landscape, however, was strictly within the Anglo-Saxon minimalist tradition.

Karkov has argued that the Anglo-Saxon portrayal of landscape tends to be 'strictly formulaic; patterned lumps and hillocks, streams flowing out of classical vessels, and trees and vines that grow in patterns similar to those in decorated initials'. She points out that there are some early eleventh-century cycles of calendar illustrations that seem to mark a change in this approach. In particular, two cycles of calendar illustrations from the British Library, which have tentatively been attributed to Christ Church, Canterbury, create a visual narrative carried by human activity. 'That is land that is being landscaped, and it is the fruits of the labour of landscaping that are the primary subject of both'.[23] Most scenes in the Tapestry have a blank background, which helps to emphasize the characters and the evolving storyline. Throughout much of the Tapestry, exterior scenes have a flooring of distinctive 'cobbling', that is, a series of small interconnected convex ridges, although this is not consistently the case; in the introductory scenes and those following the landing of the Norman fleet in England, the cobbling is missing. In the absence of cobbling, exterior events take place on the flat ground which coincides with the top line of the bottom frieze. Occasionally, hilly ground is shown and is decorated with an abstract scroll design.

There are no convincing urban scenes in the Tapestry, but it seems probable that the castles with names attached to them represent whole towns. Thus, the castles of Dol, Rennes and Dinan in Brittany and Bayeux in Normandy could be a shorthand method of depicting whole towns, just as cathedrals are used in the same way on early English county maps. It is possible that the half-built castle at Hastings was performing the same function, but here other vernacular buildings are shown.

Another device the Tapestry uses is to emphasize the importance of an individual when they first appear by locating them next to an imposing building. Duke William's first appearance on the Tapestry is when he is seen next to the great tower castle at Rouen, one of the most striking buildings in the whole of the

Bayeux Tapestry. The 'cobbling' design which is normally used to depict exterior scenes; here seen immediately above the lower border.

story. In this case the status of the building underlines William's own stature and importance.

Apart from buildings, the other main landscape features are trees. The Tapestry designer was familiar with trees, plants and foliage found in contemporary illumination, and these are frequently used as visual 'punctuation' marking a change of scene or pace. Unlike modern cartoons, the narrative takes place on one level and trees are used to indicate a change of location or event. Only occasionally, for example in the scenes showing the building of the Norman invasion fleet, are trees portrayed as actual landscape features. Trees in the Tapestry follow the conventions of contemporary illuminated manuscripts, with little attempt to reflect actual flora. They normally consist of a trunk with a number of branches. Often the branches intertwine with one another to form a hatched or an interlaced pattern. In other examples, branches fan outwards or lean to one side, as if being blown by the wind. Decorative foliage is found throughout the Tapestry, largely in the upper and lower friezes; at no point does it play an active role in the narrative.

In some places the Tapestry employs visual perspective. For example, when William and Harold's armies are passing Mont-St-Michel, the mount is depicted as a smaller feature in the background. Similarly, while on a foraging expedition after the invasion fleet has landed, the houses of the village being plundered are shown behind the Norman soldiers in such a way as to imply depth of vision.

It is significant that when some sense of depth is indicated for a given moment – generally by a second or third image higher up in the picture space and hence in the background – its subject matter is identical to that in the foreground. Thus, in one scene we see two sets of workmen building boats; and soon afterwards two files of men carrying armour to the completed vessels. There is still only one narrative subject here: it is doubled up to indicate how much manpower and effort were involved.

Bayeux Tapestry. Trees, similar to those depicted on contemporary illuminated manuscripts, are used as punctuation to divide scenes; here during the negotiations to release Earl Harold from the hands of Count Guy of Ponthieu.

Bayeux Tapestry. Prows of ships of the invasion fleet before sailing attempting to show perspective.

The general lack of depth, the absence of a recessive plane, is consonant with eleventh-century canons of pictorial representation. Its positive effect is to present the subject matter to the viewer in an immediate way. We are not looking at a story unfolding at different depths into a space which recedes away from us: everything happens right in front of our eyes.

Scale fluctuates greatly from one scene to the next. Sometimes figures fill the entire picture area, other times a building or a ship does – at which point the figures have shrunk in size. Size and scale are flexible devices which the artist manipulates (as did some contemporary illuminators) to ensure that the principal subject of every moment occupies the maximum available space, subject to the need to include inscriptions. Thus, when the principal theme is sailing, boats fill the space; when it is felling trees, trees fill the space; when it is riding, horse plus rider fills the space; and when it is the interaction of men, it is they that fill it.

Bayeux Tapestry. Ploughing and harrowing from the border of the Tapestry.

A bird slinger from a depiction of the fable Farmer and Birds from St Augustine's, Canterbury. (*Cotton MS. Claudius B.iv, f.26b, British Museum*)

For the most part, the borders do not include depictions of landscape, but there are portraits of livestock – sheep and cattle – and hunting scenes. There is one distinctive scene in the lower border showing agricultural activity throughout the year, as found in many contemporary calendars. This scene features a mouldboard plough being pulled by an animal that looks, improbably, like an ass. To the right, there is a man sowing, and a horse-drawn harrow; this represents the earliest surviving picture of the harrow. Hill has suggested that the ploughing scenes are indicative of Harold's journey taking place in early spring.[24]

Stripes on the ground underneath the horse and harrow seem to represent plough ridges. Immediately to the right of the plough and harrow scene is a boy with a sling shooting at birds. This scene appears to be taken from a depiction of the fable of 'The Swallow and the Linseed' told from the bird's perspective. The swallow knows that the linseed which is being sown will grow into flax plants that will be harvested and used for making nets to snare birds.[25]

Bayeux Tapestry. Bird slinger from the tapestry's border, see p. 17.

There is a marked contrast between the landscape evoked during the section of the Tapestry leading up to the Battle of Hastings and the battle scenes themselves. The pre-battle scenes are accompanied and punctuated by buildings and trees throughout. There is a clear attempt to create an environment against which events take place; this changes immediately the battle starts. Throughout the whole final quarter of the story no building and only a single tree is portrayed, sitting on a hill defended by the English; otherwise the background is blank. It is true that there is underfoot cobbling throughout most of the battle, but the absence of landscape features creates a stark, uninterrupted environment, against which the dramatic narrative of the battle unfolds. In the earlier part of the Tapestry the pace of events is controlled by buildings and landscape features; in the battle it is the depiction of the ebb and flow of the soldiers and horses that evokes the evolving tragedy. Almost from the start of the battle the tempo of warfare is accompanied and emphasized in the lower border by the debris of conflict; a prolonged litany of corpses, armour and discarded weaponry beat out a powerful rhythm.

Bayeux Tapestry. Soldier's corpses being stripped of their armour on the frieze.

Buildings

The Tapestry is rich in architecture and depicts thirty-three buildings, ranging from Westminster Abbey church to single-storey domestic dwellings. Most of the buildings provide a physical context for the narrative and sometimes provide information about the location of a scene. A few of the buildings are used simply for embellishment or as scene dividers like the trees, but overall they convey an authenticity appropriate to the story.

Although the depictions of several of the buildings, such as Bosham Church, give the impression that the designer was familiar with the structures, it is clear that much of the architectural detail is taken from contemporary art.[26] Early medieval art was not very concerned with architectural details and there is a tendency to copy pictures from older drawings, many of them dating from antiquity. It has been argued that 'few of the buildings shown on the Tapestry can represent contemporary structures with any degree of accuracy'.[27] Other authorities claim that in the Tapestry we are not seeing 'fantasy architecture', but 'plausible' structures, providing a realistic backdrop for the events taking place in front of them.[28]

The buildings in the Bayeux Tapestry, like those in tenth- and eleventh-century manuscript illumination, are mostly schematic, with their architectural form and constructional elements greatly simplified. This adds to the difficulty of distinguishing between those attributes which may reflect 'the real world' and those which are either imaginative or traditional iconographic motifs.[29] Nevertheless, where parts of a building shown in the Tapestry still survive, a more rigorous investigation is possible. With the exception of Westminster Abbey, the Tapestry designer does not seem to have been concerned with representing an actual contemporary building. Even in the case of Westminster, there are architectural elements illustrated that were not part of the actual church fabric. The designer seems to have created many of the buildings from a varied repertoire of architectural forms found in the visual arts.

Another problem with interpreting the Tapestry buildings is that the vast majority of vernacular structures would have been built of timber and have not survived. As there are relatively few contemporary illustrations of non-ecclesiastical buildings, we therefore have to rely on the rather patchy eleventh-century archaeological record. For the most part, archaeology can only provide the footprint of wooden palaces, hunting lodges and houses in the form of postholes and timber slots. Thus, the elaborate wooden towers shown on top of the motte-and-bailey castles on the Tapestry could be pure fantasy. However, the detail shown in these towers suggests to many commentators that their images are based on first-hand knowledge of such structures.

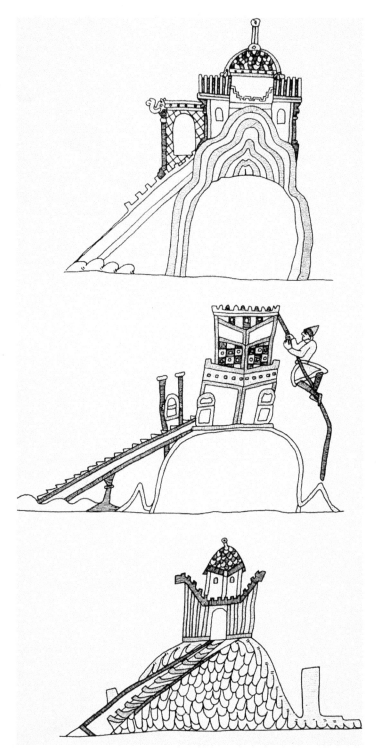

Outline drawing of the castles of Bayeux (top), Dinan and Rennet on the Bayeux Tapestry. (*Maggie Kneen*)

If the designer's basic architectural vocabulary was an inherited pictorial language, he nevertheless responded to certain aspects of the real world. Mottes, including some of the structural elements upon them, and Romanesque architectural elements are notable cases in point. It is best to remember that the Tapestry is essentially a 'cartoon', that is, it is attempting to provide a schematic visual impression of places and events. The designer uses whatever sources he or she feels necessary to convey the essential ingredients of the story. The most important factor is that the viewer should recognize what is being portrayed, without being too concerned about the detailed accuracy of the design. However, if the designer strayed too far from what the viewer was familiar with, by portraying structures that were completely alien to the observer, there would be a danger that these pictures could undermine the whole authenticity of the Tapestry.

The Roman Legacy

There are echoes of the classical world throughout the Tapestry. Many of the images are based on those from copies of classical manuscripts and others are probably taken from Trajan's Column in Rome. It is possible that other images were based on classical sculpture closer to home; for instance, the extant Porte Mars in Rheims is a reminder that much more classical imagery would have been visible in the eleventh century than today. We also know that there were many more Roman sculptural reliefs visible in the eleventh century than later. For instance the Triumphal Arch at Caerleon was only destroyed, along with the baths, in the thirteenth century. Both William and Harold would have been aware of the military importance of the Roman landscape legacy. In both Northern France and England there would have been substantial surviving Roman structures as well as a network of Roman roads, some of them serviceable. Such paved roads, even if in a dilapidated state, would have provided more direct and firmer routes for moving armies than the available local tracks and droveways. The late Saxon poem *The Ruin* portrays a decaying Romano-British city, probably Bath, and claims that the stone walls, towers and bathhouses described in the elegy were the 'work of giants'.[30]

Surviving Roman structures do not specifically feature on the Tapestry, but they would have played an important role in the events which were depicted on the hanging. When travelling to Bosham, before his fateful visit to France, Harold would probably have travelled along the Roman Stane Street between London and Chichester. Although not part of the Tapestry, the rapid movement of Harold's army to and from the Battle of Stamford Bridge would almost certainly have involved the use of Ermine Street between London and York. After the Battle of Hastings, William would have taken Watling Street from Dover to London, by way of Canterbury and Rochester. William appears to have deliberately sailed his invasion fleet to the Roman Saxon shore fort of Pevensey. This large fortified enclosure provided him with a ready-made base as soon as he landed in England, and he may later have used a similar fortification to garrison his troops at Dover.

The monks of St Augustine's would have been able to see the Roman walls of Canterbury from the abbey and were probably familiar with the Roman lighthouse at Dover and the Roman coastal forts at Richborough and Reculver. These structures, and perhaps more, would have been amongst the most impressive features in the contemporary landscape and could have influenced more of the Tapestry than we are presently aware.

Chapter 2

Earl Harold's Journey to Bosham

The first scene of the Bayeux Tapestry portrays King Edward the Confessor seated on a lion throne, addressing his brother-in-law Harold Godwinson, Earl of Wessex (c.1022–66). It appears that the king was entrusting Harold with a mission. According to Norman chroniclers the king was sending Harold to visit Duke William in Normandy in order to confirm the duke's right to the English throne on the death of the childless Confessor. William of Poitiers, William of Jumièges and Guy of Amiens (1014–1075) all agree that these events occurred in 1064 or 1065. They explain that Edward despatched Harold to William in Normandy in order to swear an oath of allegiance and to confirm William's right to the English crown when the old king died. Several sources other than the Tapestry tell of Harold undertaking a journey on behalf of the old king, but the *Anglo-Saxon Chronicle* is silent on the matter.

Bayeux Tapestry. The first scene of the Tapestry shows King Edward entrusting Earl Harold with a mission. The event takes place inside a grand building, normally interpreted as a royal palace.

As with many aspects of the story portrayed on the Tapestry, there are serious problems of interpretation. Some scholars question if such a journey ever took place and it has been argued that the story was fabricated to strengthen the legal case drawn up in 1066 to win the support of the papacy for William's proposed invasion of England. Harold was the most powerful man in Edward's kingdom, probably with regal ambitions himself. It therefore seems unlikely that he would have been willing to undertake a mission promising the crown to a rival. It seems more feasible that he went to France for quite another reason altogether, possibly to negotiate the release of two English hostages, relatives of Harold, who had been William's hostages since the early 1050s. They were Harold's youngest brother, Wulfnoth, and his nephew Hakon. Or perhaps, as others have claimed, Harold was blown off course while on naval manoeuvres in the Channel; this version of the story first appeared in Henry of Huntingdon's *Historia Anglorum* in the mid-twelfth century.

Whatever the reason for the journey, over a third of the Tapestry is devoted to the story. This includes Harold's journey to Bosham, a Channel crossing, the

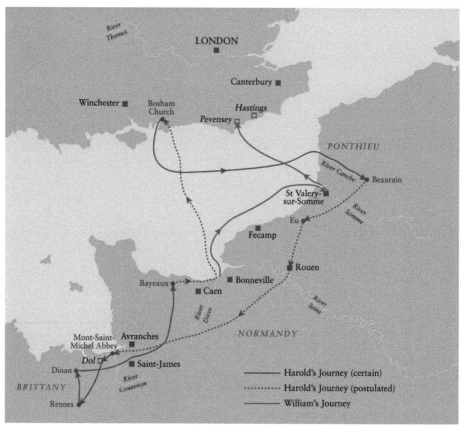

Channel crossings, plan of journeys taken by Earl Harold in 1064 and Duke William in 1066.

earl's capture and release, his journey to Rouen, his engagement in battle alongside William in the Breton campaign and the oath-taking, before returning to England. Although it is possible that several different stories have been conflated in order to create this narrative, Harold's mission is portrayed with details of people and place that suggest a degree of verisimilitude. The Tapestry is specific about a number of geographical details, notably, that Harold sailed from Bosham in Sussex and landed in Ponthieu, a considerable distance from Rouen and Caen, William's ducal power bases.

The county of Ponthieu was centred on the mouth of the River Somme and was a member of a group of vassal territories that had submitted to Duke William's overlordship after they had been defeated at the Battle of Mortemer (1054). Following the battle, Guy, the count of Ponthieu, was imprisoned for two years and obliged to swear allegiance to William.

In the eleventh century, mariners preferred to remain in sight of land if they could and would take the shortest navigable route between England and France. On the shortest Channel crossing, from Dover to the former port of Wissant, between Calais and Boulogne, land would normally have been visible at all times. It is not known where Harold landed, but he was taken to Guy's castle at Beaurain. The route from Bosham to Étaples, which was the closest seaport to Beaurain on the estuary of the River Canche, would have inevitably taken Harold's ship out of the sight of land. The Tapestry seems to confirm this, as before the arrival in Ponthieu one of the English sailors is shown at the masthead of Harold's ship looking out for land.

Harold himself had probably taken the Dover-Wissant route in 1057 when he had travelled to France and was a signatory to a charter at St Omer, which lies 40km to the east of Wissant. In 1064 Harold may have felt that it was politic to avoid Wissant, as it lay in the territory of an enemy, Eustace II, Count of Boulogne. Flanders was England's most important trading partner in the first half of the eleventh century and Gravelines, Wissant and St Omer were the primary Continental ports for Anglo-Flemish travel. In 1068 Wissant was described as a busy port filled with merchants waiting to cross to England[1] and in 1087 William Rufus sailed from Wissant to England to claim the throne on the death of his father. On the English side of the Channel, Dover, Sandwich and Hythe, in Kent, were the corresponding ports.

Harold chose to leave England from his home territory at Bosham and it would have been logical for him to have aimed to land at one of the closest French ports, which would have been Fécamp or Dieppe in Upper Normandy. It seems highly unlikely that he would have sailed from Bosham if his intended destination was indeed Ponthieu; the journey that he took would have been almost twice as long as it needed to be if he had sailed from a more conveniently sited port such as Hythe.

Most Channel crossings would have taken no more than twelve hours. Archaeological evidence in the form of pottery found in coastal ports tends to reinforce the picture painted by historical evidence, that is, that many of the cross-Channel voyages were made to ports on the immediately opposing shore. English land granted to Continental abbeys before the Conquest shows that most estates and property were sited close to a Channel port. For instance, Edward the Confessor's grants to the abbey of Fécamp included the church and land in Eastbourne, as well as land, houses and a saltern in Pevensey.[2]

Edward the Confessor's Palaces

The first scene of the Tapestry shows King Edward seated on a throne, holding a sceptre, and touching Harold's fingers in a gesture indicating trust or obligation. This scene takes place in a building with Romanesque features, almost certainly one of the king's royal palaces. During the late Saxon period the monarch had a number of palaces, which he used to visit regularly. In particular, it was the practice of the king to spend the festivals of Christmas, Easter and Whitsun at one of his palaces, possibly linked to a ceremony known as 'crown-wearing' where he presented himself in full regalia to his people.[3] By the reign of Edward the Confessor, the king's perambulations appear to have been restricted to a small group of palaces in the south and west of England, notably, Westminster, Windsor, Winchester, Wilton, near Salisbury, and Gloucester. Of the eleven known locations where Edward celebrated the three great feasts, three were at Winchester and three at Westminster, the two most important palaces in his kingdom.

Although there is no other evidence to indicate precisely where Harold's journey began, this building almost certainly represented either Westminster or

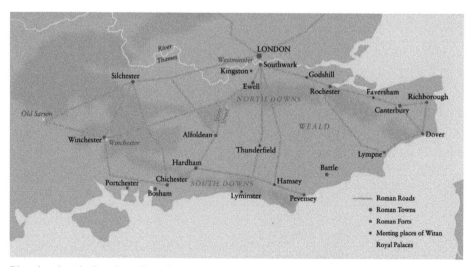

Plan showing the location of late Saxon royal palaces and meeting places of the witan in relation to Roman roads, towns and forts.

Winchester. On the other hand, the building might simply have been a generic representation of a royal residence as all of the Tapestry buildings are schematic to a degree and have been described by Lewis as 'fantasy architecture'.[4]

Royal Saxon palaces have been excavated at Yeavering, Windsor, North Elmham, Northampton, Cheddar, and Lyminge in Kent. All of these structures consist of

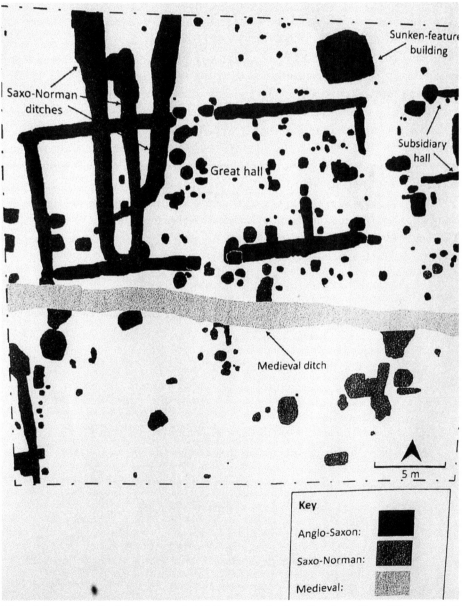

Plan of the great hall of the excavated mid-Saxon royal palace Lyminge, Kent. The great hall was the principal feature of palaces from the mid-Saxon era to the sixteenth century. (*Lyminge Archaeological Project, University of Reading*)

large wooden halls of 'post-in-trench' construction. The hall at Lyminge was built in the first half of the seventh century and has been interpreted as the core of an Anglo-Saxon royal *vill*.[5] The significant difference between these palaces and those of the eleventh century is that they were largely built of wood. All the evidence suggests that both Westminster and Winchester palaces were stone buildings, although their design, based around a large central hall, was probably similar to the earlier timber structures. The royal palaces seem to have lasted some considerable time. The palace at Cheddar, established in the ninth century, continued in use as a royal establishment until 1204, when it passed to the Bishop of Bath and Wells. Such palaces served as places of assembly, for example, the *witan* (Anglo-Saxon assembly of king's advisors) met at Cheddar in 941, 956 and 968, as well as acting as regional administrative centres for the collection of tribute and tax.

Whilst the Tapestry designer makes use of a range of basic architectural forms in the palaces, such as towers, arches, pillars and domed and pitched roofs, none of these details is exclusive to the Tapestry's aristocratic domestic buildings. The Tapestry palaces are not depicted in a consistent manner, which tends to emphasize their schematic character. For example, the royal palace building at Westminster appears on at least two occasions, but the representations are quite different in each case. Likewise, the three representations that are taken to be William's palace at Rouen seem to have little in common with each other. As far as the narrative

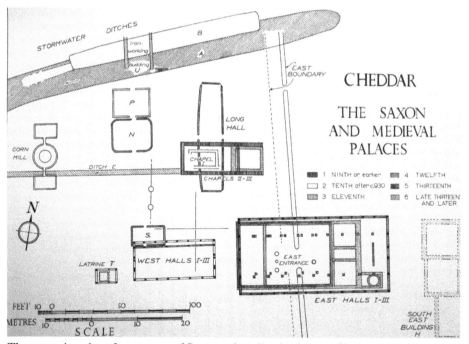

The excavation plan of a sequence of Saxon and medieval palaces at Cheddar. (*P. Rahtz*)

Early eleventh century Psalter from Canterbury. (*Harley 603, British Library*)

is concerned, such idiosyncrasies are irrelevant. Rather than replicate actual buildings, it seems that the designer has created structures from a repertoire of architectural elements found in contemporary manuscript art.

The point can be demonstrated by comparing the Tapestry's architecture with that of the Junius II manuscript of Old English poetry from Canterbury. A significant number of architectural motifs are common to both the Tapestry and this manuscript, including thin roofs supported by columns and towers. For example, the curved arches of buildings in the Tapestry have the same basic form and similar central embellishment as structures in Junius II. Similarly, the mid-level pitched roofs, domed and pointed roofs, scaled roofing, arched windows and doors, and arcading found in the Tapestry are commonly found in Junius II. The same point applies to other extensively illustrated Anglo-Saxon manuscripts, such as the Old English Hexateuch or the Harley 603 Psalter, whose illustrations were copied from an archaic Carolingian model.

Winchester

Winchester was the ancient capital of Wessex, incorporating an important royal residence, and a centre for court business and ceremonial. Anglo-Saxon kings were crowned and buried here and the palace had housed the royal treasury since at least the latter part of the reign of King Cnut (d.1035). Later in the eleventh century the city began to lose some of its former importance to London as Edward the Confessor believed that London provided a more appropriate royal capital for a monarch who was now the ruler not just of the kingdom of Wessex, but of a united England.

In addition to the palace, the south-east section of the town housed an impressive collection of ecclesiastical and monastic institutions. As a mint, Winchester was second only to London in its output of coinage, and it was the natural centre of Harold's activities as Earl of Wessex. Winchester also lay closer to the departure harbour of Bosham for Harold's Channel crossing and in that context would have been the more convenient place to meet the king. Unfortunately, we do not have a sufficiently detailed record of King Edward's movements to help identify the location, but we do know that he was still travelling around southern England late into his reign. For instance, it is recorded that Edward was hunting in Hampshire with Harold's half-brother, Tostig (c.1029–66), Earl of Northumbria, in the autumn of 1065, when they received news of an uprising in York against Tostig. There were

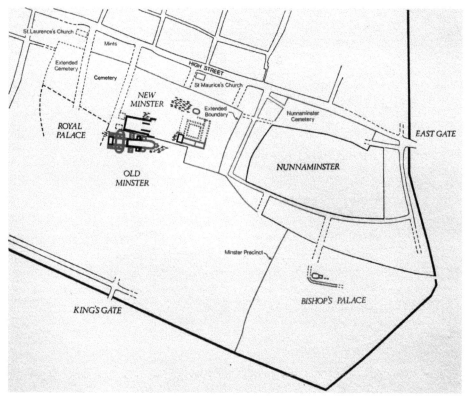

Plan showing the site of the late Saxon royal palace at Winchester in relation to the cathedral and south-east section of the walled town. (*Biddle, 1976*)

several royal hunting lodges in the region, such as those at Andover (Hampshire) or Britford, near Wilton, where Edward moved after he received the news of the northern rebellion against Tostig. Edward and Harold could have met in such a hunting lodge prior to the earl's departure, but it is unlikely that the building in the Tapestry was meant to represent anything other than one of the great royal palaces.

The palace at Winchester was the principal royal residence of the Anglo-Saxon kings and probably dated from the tenth century and was sited in the heart of the walled city. Winchester was the older of the two main royal palaces, but relatively little is known about the late Saxon royal residence there. Documentary evidence suggests that the palace lay to the west of the present cathedral (and the old minster). Martin Biddle interprets the site of Saxon power as being in the same location as it had been in Roman Winchester, 'a site in or adjacent to the basilica of the forum, just to the west and north of the present cathedral', within 40m (130ft) of the west front of the seventh-century church. Probably, the palace underlies the western part of the medieval graveyard.[6]

It has been argued that the site was originally chosen for a royal hall by early West Saxon kings both to utilize existing building material and possibly to associate their rule with former Roman authority.[7] Undoubtedly, the palace had some stone buildings, but there is a complete absence of archaeological evidence relating to its layout and appearance. If the palace depicted on the Tapestry represents the

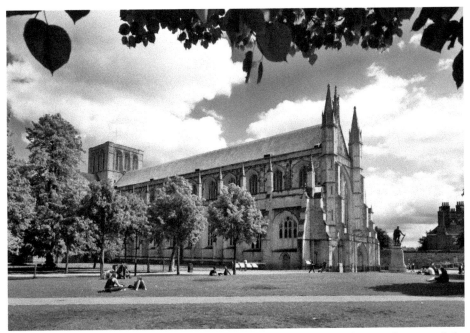

Winchester Cathedral showing the probable location of the royal palace to the west of the cathedral (right of photograph).

late Saxon royal residence at Winchester, it is the only surviving evidence for its appearance.

It is probable that late Saxon kings used Winchester Palace for the ceremony of 'crown-wearing', which had almost certainly originated before the Conquest. In 1086 this event was described as the occasion when 'the king wore his royal crown three times a year at Easter at Winchester, at Whitsuntide at Westminster, at Christmas at Gloucester'. On these occasions 'all the great men of England were assembled about' the king and such palaces were appropriate for other ceremonial events, notably, the marriage and coronation of queens.[8]

About 1070 William the Conqueror extended the enclosure of the original palace north to Winchester High Street and doubled it in size. The new precinct took in the new minster cemetery, destroyed twelve houses and five *monete* (workshops associated with a mint) and blocked off a street. He built a palace and a hall in the new enclosure, which was described by Gerald the Welshman at the end of the twelfth century as second neither in quality nor in quantity to Westminster. It is not known if any of the Saxon palace was demolished at this time.[9]

William the Conqueror also built a castle at the western end of the walled area of the city, but he continued to use his new palace and celebrated Easter there on at least five occasions. During the first half of the twelfth century, royal patronage of the Winchester palace declined and eventually it was taken over by the Bishop of Winchester. In 1138 Bishop Henry of Blois added a keep to the palace, but just three years later the city of Winchester was burnt and the palace was partly destroyed. A later chronicler recounts how the bishop used this opportunity to demolish what was left of the Saxon palace on the grounds that it lay too close to the cathedral, subsequently reusing the building materials for his own new residence at the Wolvesey Palace in the south-east corner of the walled city.[10]

Westminster

Despite Winchester's closer proximity to Bosham, it is likely that Harold's party left from Westminster, which was being developed as a grand royal centre by Edward the Confessor, near to the capital of a recently united England. There had been a late Saxon royal residence in the walled city of London in the Cripplegate-Aldermanbury area, but this structure was inadequate for Edward's purposes and consequently he established a new royal palace on Thorney Island, from which he could supervise the building of his new abbey. Thorney Island lay on the north bank of the River Thames about 2km upstream from the walled city of London. Even on the new site there was a shortage of space. Indeed the narrow strip of low, damp ground, about 91.5m (300ft) wide, squeezed between the abbey and the river, was an extraordinary site on which to locate the chief palace of the kings of England.[11] There appears to have been an earlier church dating from the eighth century dedicated to St Peter here, and this in turn might have been built on the site of a Romano-British temple dedicated to Apollo. The Roman material found at Westminster has recently been reassessed by Henig, who has argued that there may have been a Romano-British villa and cemetery on the site. A fourth-century sarcophagus was found here in the nineteenth century; its lid was later refashioned and carved with a Latin cross in the tenth or eleventh century. Henig suggests that this lid plus other Roman material recorded in the vicinity could have belonged to a mausoleum or *martyrium* that was subsequently incorporated into an early Saxon church. The site may then have acquired special sanctity in a similar way to the Gallo-Roman cemetery outside Paris that contained the *martyrium* of St Denis and which eventually, like Westminster, became a royal abbey.[12] St Peter's became known as the West Minster while St Paul's, lying to the east, was known as the East Minster. It has been suggested that Edward chose Westminster as a secluded location for his palace after a confrontation with anti-Norman nobles in the city in 1052.[13]

Westminster Abbey had been founded or refounded as a Benedictine house by St Dunstan during the reign of King Edgar (AD 959–975) in *c*.AD 971.[14] As Archbishop of Canterbury, Dunstan was responsible for a monastic revival in England. This building was described as a *monasterollum* (little monastery), inhabited by an abbot and twelve monks. This account of Dunstan's abbey dates from *c*.1086 and may have deliberately understated the size of the earlier institution in order to promote the importance of Edward's new structure. The account of Westminster in the *Life of King Edward* extols the virtues of the location: 'It both lay by the famous and

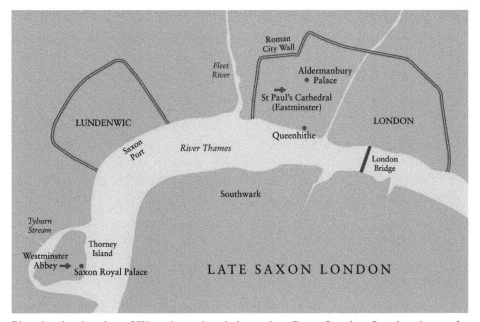

Plan showing location of Westminster in relation to late-Saxon London. Lundenwic was the site of early/mid-Saxon London.

rich town and also was a delightful spot surrounded with fertile lands and green fields and near the main channel of the river which bore abundant merchandise of wares of every kind for sale from the whole world'. The relationship between the abbey church and the Tapestry is discussed in Chapter 6.

Excavations in advance of the London Underground Jubilee line extension project in the 1990s provided further evidence of Edward's palace. One structure found was in the form of a revetment consisting of badly decayed wooden planks, almost 2m long, attached to a series of wooden posts between 60mm and 100mm in diameter and up to 9m in length. This structure has been interpreted as a bridge linked to the palace. The dendrochronology data points to a date AD 970–1050, which was slightly earlier than Edward's building, suggesting there having been an important structure on the site even before his. It has also been proposed that Cnut (1016–35) could have resided on the site.[15] It would appear that at the same time a wide boundary ditch was dug, possibly also with a bridge constructed over it. This defined the land that was to become the site of the Royal Palace of Westminster.[16] The Jubilee line extension excavations did not prove that there was a palace at Westminster before Edward the Confessor, but they demonstrated that its site had been defined with a substantial boundary or defence and that there was earlier occupation here. In the 1950s a large ditch was excavated on the south side of the abbey, cutting through deep layers of fluvial sediments, suggesting that the whole area of the abbey was subject to severe flooding over many centuries. A gravel road laid over these silts may have provided access to construction work within the precinct. The backfilled ditch contained large amounts of pottery showing the transition between late Saxon wares and Anglo-Norman ceramics.[17]

A priceless opportunity to find out more about Edward's palace at Westminster was missed in the 1970s, when an underground car park was dug for Members of Parliament. 'It is one of the scandals of modern British archaeology that no large-scale archaeological excavation was undertaken to recover the plan of Edward the Confessor's palace' at that time.[18] Following the Ancient Monuments and Archaeological Areas Act 1979 and subsequent legislation, archaeological assessment has become a mandatory feature of most proposed redevelopment projects and hopefully ensured that such an opportunity would not be missed in the future. Although the precise site of Edward's palace is still not certain, it is generally believed that it occupied the site later called the 'lesser hall' or the 'white hall'.

During the 1050s, Westminster became one of the principal royal residences and would have been the location for crown-wearing on a number of occasions.[19] King Harold and the court were gathered for Easter at Westminster Palace in April 1066 when Halley's Comet was sighted.

The palace lay immediately to the south of the Great Hall, built by William Rufus at the end of the eleventh century, and east of Edward's own abbey church.

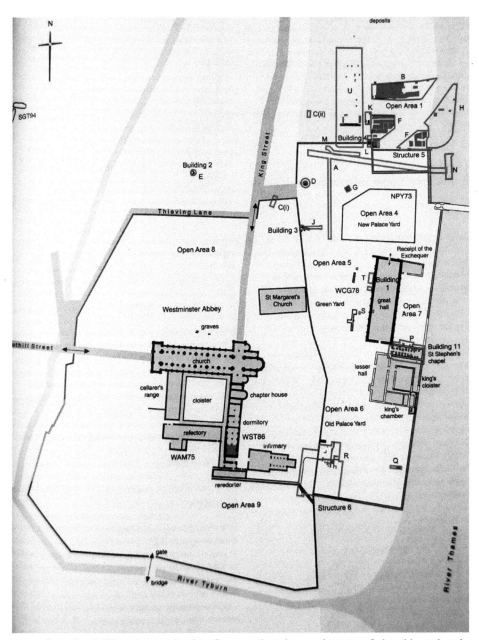

Plan of medieval Westminster, the late-Saxon palace lay to the east of the abbey church, probably on the site of the lesser hall. (*Thomas2002*)

It occupied the area to the north of the House of Lords, marked by the Victorian statue of Richard the Lionheart.

The inspiration for the royal complex, incorporating abbey and palace, seems to have come from the ducal site of Fécamp in Upper Normandy, where the abbey

The statue of Richard the Lionheart to the north of the Houses of Parliament, roughly occupying the site of Edward the Confessor's palace at Westminster.

and palace shared a common enclosure. Westminster was intended as a private royal church and mausoleum, like the Carolingian *Eigenkloster* and royal Saint-Denis of the French kings. Edward must have believed that such a royal complex, close to his capital city, would place him on an equal level to his European imperial and regal counterparts.

The palace was a single-storey building with a screened passage at the northern end; thus, the northern section would have been used for the preparation of food before it was taken into the main dining area. In front of the building there was a small fountain or washing area. The king's chamber with the king's bed may have been in a separate building.[20]

The grand edifice depicted on the left of the opening action on the Tapestry might be a separate building to the palace; but more probably represents its entrance. This feature is depicted in the form of a two-storey structure with an upper gallery above which there are three windows and a decorated conical roof. Around the doorway is an area of lozenge-pattern decoration that is repeated in the form of squares around the windows on the first floor. In front of the entrance there are three steps, and the structure is framed by towers on either side. This grand architectural statement at the very beginning of the Tapestry has been interpreted as a portal which 'draws the viewer ... along on the narrative journey'.[21]

Bayeux Tapestry.
Portal to Westminster
Palace providing a
grand beginning to the
Tapestry.

Palaces in England are depicted elsewhere in the Tapestry: for example, when Harold reports to Edward on his return to England, on Edward's death, and when Harold is crowned king. Palatial buildings are also shown in Normandy on several occasions. There is no consistency in their architectural features, although some architectural elements are emphasized, possibly to provide a clue as to the building's location.

The Road to Bosham

After Harold and his *milites* (supporting soldiers) leave the king's palace, they are shown riding to Bosham, the earl's estate in Sussex. If Harold's party travelled from Westminster they probably took the Stane Street, a Roman road running between London and Chichester. Stane Street was one of six hard-surfaced roads built from London by the Romans and much of it would still have been in use in the late Saxon period; for much of its length it can be clearly traced today.

Bayeux Tapestry. Earl Harold holding a hunting bird, accompanied by hunting dogs on the way to Bosham.

The Westminster-Bosham (*c*.100km) route would have taken about three days and involved crossing the North and South Downs and part of the Weald. There were few settlements of any size along the road, but on the way down the earl could have stopped at Ewell, a royal estate, or Dorking, which was in the hands of his sister Queen Edith, and at Hardham, a small estate, south-west of Pulborough, of which he was lord.

The shorter journey from Winchester to Bosham (*c*.50km) would have taken up to two days, but it is not clear which route Harold would have taken. The Roman road between Winchester and Chichester has disappeared, and although stretches of it have been identified through fieldwork, there is no evidence that it was still in use at this date. There would have been a functioning Roman road between Winchester and Portchester (Romano-British *Portus Adurni*) and this is likely to have been the preferred route in the late Saxon period. After Portchester, travellers would have moved eastwards along the coast to Bosham and Chichester.

The Hunt

Either route would have involved some serious riding, but Harold's party looks as if it is setting out for the hunt rather than embarking on a long journey. Harold holds a hawk or falcon with a strap and is accompanied by a pack of three hunting dogs wearing collars and bells. The hounds are chasing small game, possibly hares, which appear to be entering a wood, represented by a single tree. Providing service to the king or one's lord at the hunt was as important as military service in late Saxon England and this scene demonstrates the significance of hunting to the Saxon aristocracy. The Anglo-Saxon chronicler Eadmer of Canterbury (*c*.1060–*c*.1126) noted that living like an earl meant 'keeping horses and going hunting with hawks and hounds'. This conspicuous display of a hunting bird is a symbol of Harold's high aristocratic status.

This scene shows Harold's party hunting while on its way to the coast or depicts a hunt that took place after its arrival at Bosham. Another interpretation is that Harold was taking the hunting dogs and hawk as gifts for Duke William. The Tapestry designer appears to have copied the hunting scene from similar illustrations found on contemporary calendars, for instance, the dogs are similar to those that appear in the Eadwine Psalter (*c*.1150) from Canterbury.[22] The hunting

Hunt scene on Romanesque capital, Goult Priory, Orne, Normandy. Hunting is an activity regularly depicted on eleventh-century carving and in illuminated manuscripts. This particular image may have been copied from a classical source.

theme is also found in church architecture, for instance: there is a Romanesque capital from the early twelfth-century abbey at Vézelay in Burgundy which depicts a hunting scene. Hunting scenes, such as the deer hunt at Gosforth, Cumbria, also appear regularly on Saxon and Scandinavian crosses in northern Britain.

Conventionally, hunting has been associated with William the Conqueror and the Normans. In particular, the introduction of royal forests and Forest Law has been seen as an expression both of the duke's 'love of the chase' and the Normans' ruthless suppression of Saxon rights. Recent research into the hunting activities of the Saxons suggests that hunting was already an important activity for late Saxon monarchs and a recognized aristocratic pastime. Both Cnut and Edward the Confessor had reserved hunting areas, but they did not claim exclusive rights as Norman kings did when they created Royal Forests. Edward is recorded as having hunting reserves and lodges on his demesne land; he also employed wardens and huntsmen in several areas that later became royal forest.[23] There is a significant rise in the volume of bones from deer and other wild animals of the chase on high-status late Anglo-Saxon archaeological sites such as Bishopstone (Sussex).[24]

The English Chronicler William of Malmesbury (c.1095–c.1143) records that Edward the Confessor's sole worldly pleasure was his love of birds and hounds, which he inspected daily after mass. He added that Edward particularly loved the sport of hawking: 'There was one earthly enjoyment in which he chiefly delighted which was hunting with fleet hounds whose opening in the woods he used with pleasure to encourage; and again with the pouncing of birds, whose nature it is to prey on their kindred species. To these sports he would devote himself for days on end'. Although hunting was a regular pastime of kings and nobles, the sport was prohibited to clergy by canon law and never regarded by the church as completely respectable. Edward's apparent addiction to the chase appears to contradict the saintly persona which is normally attributed to him. He could have acquired this passion during his time spent in Normandy, but it is also possible that in Edward's case it was used to establish the king's 'simplicity'.

Domesday Book (1086) records that the counties of Wiltshire, Oxfordshire and Northamptonshire and the city of Leicester each owed the king £10 a year for a hawk, and the county of Worcestershire owed £10 for a Norway hawk (probably a peregrine falcon). All these obligations were accompanied by payments for a packhorse and three were associated with payments 'for dogs'. The Northamptonshire payment included 20s for a horse for the huntsman.[25] Harold may also have been keen on hawking and falconry and, in a discussion about hunting birds, Adelard of Bath (in the twelfth century) noted that the earl kept a collection of books on the subject. In 1065 Harold 'ordered some building to be done at Portskewet (Wales) … and there he got together many goods and thought of having King Edward for hunting'. The venture was cut short as several of Harold's workmen were killed during an attack by the Welsh prince, Caradog ap Gruffyd (d.1081).[26]

Bayeux Tapestry. Detail of huntsman with dogs on border.

The Saxon kings did not reserve areas of England for their own exclusive hunting, but they did have favourite royal hunting localities over which they established a degree of control. For example, some elements of William the Conqueror's New Forest in Hampshire were already in existence in King Edward's time.[27] Similarly, it now appears that deer parks, long thought to be a Norman innovation, were in existence before 1066. Domesday Book records two deer parks belonging to Bosham Church and several others owned by different landholders in the vicinity of Bosham. There is increasing evidence to show that such parks were created before 1066. Aristocratic families, such as the Godwinsons, would have been able to hunt in parks created by clients and friends in the region around Bosham and Chichester.[28] Harold and his men would have hunted regularly in the region and could well have done so on this occasion, prior to their departure for France.[29] Domesday Book also records a royal hunting park near to Hastings, at Rotherfield.

There is one other depiction of hunting dogs and falcons in the main Tapestry narrative, when Harold is seen accompanying Duke William back to his palace in Rouen. The duke had several parks in the vicinity of Rouen and it is possible that during Harold's visit to the duchy the two went hunting together.

Bosham Harbour

The text above the hunt scene in the Tapestry observes, 'Where Harold, Earl of the English, and his army ride to Bosham church'. The next scene shows Harold

Bayeux Tapestry. Earl Harold entering Bosham church, adjacent to the hall.

and a companion entering the church. Bosham lies on a branch of Chichester Harbour, about 5km (3 miles) to the west of Chichester, and had for long been one of the principal points of departure for Channel crossings The church and ancient harbour at Bosham occupy a spur between two tidal channels that run inland. Bosham Church lies directly in line with the last 1.5km of the navigable channel in Bosham Creek and would have been used as a landmark for navigation purposes. It has been argued that it may have been located here in the first place for that reason.[30] It has also been suggested that the church nave might have been used for drying sails, as was the practice in some tenth-century Norwegian churches.

The harbour was regularly used by the Godwinson family. Swein Godwinson's ships were lying in Bosham harbour when he kidnapped and murdered his cousin Bjorn in 1049, and it was from Bosham harbour that the Godwinsons fled to exile in Bruges in 1051. Bosham was the centre for the Godwines' fleet and probably an important shipbuilding centre as well. To sustain this role it would have had a range of facilities, including storehouses, repair shops and an area for ship construction. The manor of Bosham encompassed the Chidham peninsula, which also lay in Chichester Harbour and had several advantages for the harbouring and protection of longships. In addition, the manor of Thorney Island (Sussex) was also associated with the maritime activities of Bosham and in 1086 was a member of the Chapel of Bosham. Prior to collecting the Godwinsons from Thorney Island in 1051, the vessels that took them to Flanders are described as being held at Bosham and 'launched' from the island. Thorney Island was detached from the mainland in the Middle Ages and was still shown as an island in Chichester Harbour on Saxton's map of Sussex in 1575.

Bosham

Bosham was one of Harold's favourite residences and his chief seat, where he had a grand hall, a private fleet and a harbour; his father, Godwin, first Earl of Wessex (1001–1053), had established an important minster church here. The earl's estate here consisted of fifty-six and a half hides in 1066 according to Domesday Book. Woodland yielding six swine was also recorded and may relate to Old Park Wood, a surviving place name which could refer to a medieval hunting park.[31] Domesday Book records that the western portion of the Bosham estate belonged to the church and was given by Edward the Confessor to his Norman chaplain Osbern, who became Bishop of Exeter after the Conquest. The remainder belonged to Earl Harold.

On the Tapestry, the church and hall are shown together and are roughly the same size; one commentator has suggested that this might reflect the equal division of the minster's resources between church and earl.[32] Harold is shown entering the church with a colleague, both are bending their knees; perhaps indicating that they were going to pray for a safe Channel crossing. Subsequently, the earl and his party are depicted feasting in an elaborate two-storey building immediately prior to their departure for France.

Bosham is one of only four places in England to be named on the Tapestry. The early chroniclers do not identify the place from which Harold embarked and it

Bayeux Tapestry. Feast in upper storey of *logia* before embarking on the channel crossing.

is not until the late twelfth century that sources other than the Tapestry record Bosham in this context. One explanation for the specific naming of Bosham is that it was associated with the Godwinsons' earlier disloyalty to King Edward and a comparison was being made with Harold's perjury in relation to Duke William. Harold's pious entry to the church on bended knee may have been read as typical Godwinson hypocrisy.

The village of Bosham lies close to the Romano-British palace of Fishbourne and the Roman town of *Noviomagus Reginorum* (Chichester). Not surprisingly, Roman material has been found around the village, but the nature of the Roman settlement here is unknown. Bosham was mentioned in Bede's *Ecclesiastical History* (*c*.731) in connection with the conversion of Sussex to Christianity. Bede records St Wilfred visiting a pre-existing small Celtic monastery, said to be 'surrounded by woods and the sea', which was occupied by a monk called Dicul and five or six brethren in AD 681.

Holy Trinity Church in Bosham is comparable in scale with other Saxon churches in Sussex, such as Stoughton. The west tower reaches up to almost 17m (56ft) in height and in the eleventh century it was one of the richest churches in England.[33]

The interpretation of the archaeology of the present church of Holy Trinity has been hotly disputed, although there is universal agreement that some of the building, at least, is pre-1066. Gem has recently argued that parts of the church

View of Bosham church from a boathouse on the waterfront.

Exterior of Holy Trinity church, Bosham.

could be much earlier than previously thought and date to the seventh or eighth century, not long after St Wilfred's visit. On the other hand, he believes that the chancel arch, for long seen as a pre-Conquest feature, actually dates from around 1070.[34] In either case, it could have been built before the Tapestry was executed.

The portrayal of Bosham Church on the Tapestry has been the subject of much speculation as it is one of the few buildings that still bears some resemblance today to how it appears on the Tapestry. It is depicted as a rectangular building with a trapezoid pitched roof and a cross at either end. It has a large central rounded arch, which has been interpreted by some as a representation of the extant chancel arch. Musset has argued that the dimensions of the chancel arch match the proportions of the embroidered image.[35] Conversely it has recently been claimed that the Bosham arch on the Tapestry is actually a door.[36] Immediately under the roof there are nine small round-headed windows and on either side of the central arch there are slender, pointed turrets. Musset argues that apart from the central arch there is little attempt at realism or perspective: 'But these interpretive difficulties simply reflect the limitations of the medium: emphasis on a key feature has to take precedence over any attempt at an accurate overall view'.

Others have argued that there is no direct relationship between the late Saxon church at Bosham and its depiction on the Tapestry and that the architectural features displayed, such as the round arched windows and doorways, were typical features of many late Anglo-Saxon churches. For example, the arcade of

Bayeux Tapestry. Detail of the church at Bosham, Earl Harold and a companion are entering the building from the north side, their knees are bent. There appear to be steps on either side of the building.

windows below the roofline is similar to that at St Lawrence, Bradford-on-Avon. In other words, along with all the other buildings on the Tapestry, it is a schematic representation of an actual building and it is possible that the designer had never seen Bosham Church.[37]

Hart has argued that Bosham Church was inspired by a shrine of St Mildred from St Augustine's, Canterbury, and there are clearly similarities between the two structures. However, as both are Romanesque, they would inevitably share some common characteristics.[38]

Various historical myths are associated with the church at Bosham. One suggests that a carving in an arch of the north wall of the chancel represents a daughter of King Cnut; despite general agreement that the sculpture is fourteenth century, an associated story claimed that the episode of Cnut's attempting to turn back the waves occurred at Bosham. A second persistent myth is that King Harold was buried here, although there is no evidence to support this whatsoever.

Romanesque chancel arch at Holy Trinity Bosham. Many believe that this structure is depicted on the Tapestry.

St Lawrence, Bradford on Avon, late Saxon church with a blind round-arched arcade found on several of the buildings depicted on the Tapestry.

Immediately to the right of the church a grand secular building is depicted on the Tapestry. It has been suggested that this two-storey structure could have been part of an ecclesiastical complex at Bosham, but it is more likely to have been Harold's hall or lodge. According to the Tapestry, the building is by the harbour as the outside staircase leads directly down to the beach for embarkation. The steep rake of the beach and the rapid rise of the tide at Bosham are still evident today, where streets adjacent to the harbour are flooded at high tide on a daily basis. The ground floor of the Bosham building on the Tapestry is open to the elements and consists of three large semicircular arches carried by columns with moulded capitals. The Tapestry provides no clue to its function, but it may well have been used for storage or for the stabling of horses. The first floor is being used as a banqueting hall which runs the whole length of the building and is covered by a sloping roof consisting of coloured tiles. The structure was probably a *laubia* or lodge, of the type frequently mentioned in medieval documents. According to the Tapestry, the chamber in which Edward dies is also sited on the first floor of his Westminster palace. The *Anglo-Saxon Chronicle* for 978 describes the collapse of an upper timber floor under the weight of the royal council, assembled in the king's palace at Calne (Wiltshire) in what was called a *solarium;* only Dunstan, the Archbishop of Canterbury (d.988), managed to survive the resulting carnage unscathed by standing on a beam.

The first-floor post-Conquest halls at Richmond Castle and Castle Acre have a similar design to the building depicted on the Tapestry and differ only in that they are stone rather than wooden constructions. At Richmond (North Yorkshire) there is an elegant late eleventh-century first-floor hall sited within the confines of a triangular perimeter wall. At Castle Acre, also from the late eleventh century, there was a low earthwork surmounted by two semi-detached, parallel first-floor halls, called 'a country house' by the excavator.[39] The hall-castle at Chepstow (Gwent), built immediately after the Conquest, used a developed form of this design. The present manor house at Bosham was built in the mid-seventeenth century, but reputedly was constructed from the remains of an ancient structure that stood near the site.[40]

Excavations carried out in the 1990s at Vintners' Place on the former Thames waterfront in London immediately to the north of Southwark Bridge uncovered a tenth-century timber structure that bears a certain resemblance to the Bosham building.[41] By the mid-eleventh century, many castles (in France) were equipped with rectangular halls, with the hall sitting over some form of basement. Access to the upper storey was usually by means of an external staircase, normally constructed of timber. As early as 950 there was a building of this type, belonging

Boothby Pagnell manor, Lincs. late twelfth century first floor hall and solar set above a vaulted two chamber undercroft. An external stairway leads to the first floor.

Interior of the great hall at Chepstow Castle. Historically this building has been attributed to William FitzOsbern but it is now believed to have been the work of William the Conqueror himself. The re-use of material from the nearby Romano-British town of Caerwent (*Venta Silurum*) together with the deliberate use of Roman architectural features suggest that this was intended as an 'imperial' statement of intent, by the king on the boundary of Wales. (*Turner* et al *2006, 37–42*)

to Count Theobald of Blois, at Doué-la-Fontaine (Maine-et-Loire). The castle at Brionne (Haute-Normandie), which was besieged by William the Conqueror between 1047 and 1050, was 'a stone-built hall serving the defenders as a keep'.[42]

The hall at Bosham probably continued to be used by high-status travellers prior to their departure across the Channel as a 'glorified waiting room, with banquets ... served to the royal travellers as they awaited the correct wind and tide'.[43]

On the Tapestry the figures on the first floor are seated and drinking from large horns and cups. The drinking horns appear to be of a typical Saxon variety and are made of ox horn with possible gold decoration around the rim. By the mid-eleventh century such oschaic drinking horns had become symbols of vanity and sin and their use may have been used to indicate the 'moral lassitude' of the English.[44] The nature of the lively Bosham feast has been compared with the more solemn banquet overseen by Bishop Odo, held before the Battle of Hastings. It was probably a banquet or ceremony of departure or leave-taking of the type that occurred in many contemporary stories, part of the rituals associated with assuring a safe journey. Such symbolic feasts marking the start of journey or a battle can be traced back as far as the Homeric epics of the Greek Bronze Age.

Two of Harold's party are pointing towards the sea and are already leaving the hall, perhaps indicating that the party has gone on too long and that the tide is changing. As Harold's group embarks they descend the steps from the upper floor of the *loggia* directly into the sea. A precise division between land and water is apparent at the foot of the steps, where two of the men are barelegged and wading out through the wavy lines depicting the sea, while one of the men is still wearing trousers and shoes and is standing on one side of a line which demarcates the boundary between sea and shore.

Earl Harold's contingent moves from the feast to the waiting boat. One of the men holds a hunting dog, while others hold oars and a curious bent device, perhaps used for determining wind direction.

Chapter 3

Earl Harold in France

A fter leaving Bosham the Tapestry shows Harold and his contingent sailing across the English Channel. On landing in France they are immediately confronted by Guy, Count of Ponthieu, who arrests the earl and holds him to ransom. Harold is freed through the intervention of Duke William and travels to Rouen. Subsequently, William, accompanied by the English party, takes an army into the Breton Marches, where a series of castles are attacked. At the end of the campaign William awards Harold his arms, and on returning to Normandy Harold swears an oath in the presence of William at Bayeux. The earl then sails back to England.

According to the Tapestry Harold's entourage sailed from Bosham in a single ship. Apart from a line of English round shields outside the gunwale, there are no arms or supplies to be seen. Additionally, no horses are depicted, although a hunting dog and falcon are shown being carried on board prior to the departure

Bayeux Tapestry. This scene shows Harold's ship sailing to France in 1064. The earl is at the helm.

from Bosham harbour. The basic form of the ships depicted on the Tapestry is typical of eleventh-century Anglo-Norman design, which was derived from Viking longships.

Archaeological evidence for early medieval ships is rare in Britain, but vessels such as the early seventh-century ship from Mound 1 at Sutton Hoo (Suffolk) and the tenth-century boat from Graveney (Kent) are basically the same as those seen on the Tapestry. There is considerably more evidence of maritime activity from Scandinavia for this period, including a group of five boats excavated near Skuldelev, Denmark. These had been scuttled in the eleventh century to block the Roskilde fjord, with the intention of protecting the royal town of Roskilde from attack by sea. These wrecks are particularly valuable as they constitute a variety of vessels ranging from small traders to warships. One of these boats had been built in Dublin, using local timber.[1]

The surviving physical evidence suggests that eleventh-century ships generally followed the Viking model. Clinker built, the hull was symmetrical, with the keel rounding gently into curved stem posts. Strakes would have been fastened with

Reconstruction of an excavated Viking ship from Roskilde, Denmark. (*McGrail 1983*)

Wooden animal head post from the
Oseberg ship burial, Norway (AD 834).
Such posts probably had some ritual
significance. Their design was adapted
for the figureheads of Viking ships.

iron clench nails or wooden pegs and caulked with tarred animal hair. The gunwale
had a distinctive curve, significantly lower amidships. Internally, the hull was
supported with frames and beam knees. Although some vessels had decking fore
and aft, most would have been open to the elements. Many ships were propelled
by a single square sail, whilst others would have been rowed or used a combination
of both methods. Oars were worked from rowlocks or oar ports. Ships would have
been steered by a rudder from the starboard quarter, which often would have been
fixed and operated using a tiller.[2] Such vessels were sleek, narrow in the beam,
shallow-drafted and could move very quickly.

Harold's ship had a carved figurehead at the prow and at the stern as well.
Figureheads of beasts and kings are well attested in literary sources although
archaeological evidence for them is relatively rare. It is possible that the heads,
which might have been intended to depict status or intimidate, were removed
when landing in friendly territory, but there is no evidence of this practice on the
Tapestry. Harold's boat was propelled both by sail and by oars, the holes for which
are shown on one of the images. The sail mast was lowered when landing. The
helmsman was also the captain. In this case it was Earl Harold himself who steered
the ship with a large wooden batten or oar, attached to the right-hand side at the

stern of the boat. The helmsman was also responsible for adjusting the tightness of the sail. In the Tapestry the sail is shown in a curved, triangular form, which it has been argued is a stylized version of a square sail.[3]

Ponthieu

If we accept the Tapestry's version of events, Harold's ship did not land in Normandy. It came ashore to the north of the River Somme in Ponthieu, a territory that had been created as a marcher territory at the western extremity of the Carolingian Empire and whose function would have been to guard the Somme estuary. Like the Normans to the south, the counts of Ponthieu enjoyed a large measure of independence, but in 1054 Count Guy had joined the French king and rebellious Norman barons in a war against Duke William. At the Battle of Mortemer in February 1054, Guy was captured and subsequently imprisoned for two years in Bayeux. During that time he would have become acquainted with William's half-brother Bishop Odo of Bayeux, who may even have been charged with the responsibility of guarding the count. The significance given to Guy in the Tapestry could, therefore, be the result of a friendship between the two men, which is reflected by Odo as the sponsor of the Tapestry.

Count Guy had been obliged to declare himself William's vassal, but this did not prevent him from arresting Harold and negotiating with the duke for the earl's

Bayeux Tapestry. Count Guy on horseback arrests Earl Harold on his landing in Ponthieu.

release. Holding Harold to ransom may have been a means for Guy to retaliate for his imprisonment by the duke, although only two years later the count was almost certainly part of William's army at the Battle of Hastings.

There is no indication from the Tapestry precisely where Harold's party came ashore, either pictorially or in the text. All that is shown is the boat beaching and an anchor on the shore, where Harold is arrested by Guy of Ponthieu even before the earl has left the water.

Several of the chroniclers confirm that Harold did land in Ponthieu and William of Poitiers claimed that Harold was seized by Count Guy 'according to the barbarous customs of the country, as if he were a shipwrecked mariner'. It was a common practice for wealthy nobles to be held hostage if they strayed into territories where they were not welcome or indeed if their arrival was unexpected. One likely landing place would have been somewhere in the Somme estuary, possibly even at Saint-Valery-sur-Somme, from where Duke William's invasion fleet was to embark two years later. Alternatively, they could have landed at Étaples, a port lying at the mouth of the River Canche. The Canche estuary, along with those of the other French Channel rivers, the Somme, Authie, Bresle and Béthune, then ran much further inland than it does today. Montreuil-sur-Mer, which now lies 16km from the coast, was a prosperous medieval river port and the Canche was probably navigable even further upstream. It is even possible that Harold was transported upstream by boat as far as Beaurain, where he was held by Guy.

The Frankish emporium of Quentovic, whose name means 'the market on the Canche', also lay in the Canche Valley. This was an important trading port in the eighth to tenth centuries and seems to have been particularly popular with pilgrims who crossed the English Channel. After Viking attacks it was abandoned in the eleventh century in favour of more easily fortified sites nearby. The precise location of Quentovic has been a matter of dispute, but fieldwork by Hill placed it on the Canche just to the north-west of Montreuil in what is now the commune of La Calotterie.[4]

The appearance of Guy of Ponthieu marks the first case of right to left movement in the Tapestry. The fact that he appears from the other direction and is followed by a group of four knights also moving to the left emphasizes that he is obstructing Harold's progress and arresting him. The technique is used with similar effectiveness to express the meeting of Harold, Guy and William, where William and three companions ride from right to left; and again for Harold's encounter with Edward when he finally returns to England.

The only clues the Tapestry provides about the topography of this region of north-west France through which Harold travelled are the buildings. Apart from the coast, the only landscape features are the usual trees used as punctuation to divide the various episodes. One of the trees has a rocky feature around the base of its trunk, but its function or symbolism if any is unclear.

Aerial view of Count Guy's castle at Beaurain. This substantial earthwork castle is largely hidden by dense tree cover, but it occupies the apex of the woodland in the centre of the photograph.

Harold and his entourage, including hunting dogs and hawk, are taken to Guy's castle or palace at a place called Belrem (Beaurainville), which sits on a low hill overlooking the Canche Valley. Although a prisoner, Harold would have been treated as an important guest. The building at 'Belrem', into which the earl enters to meet Guy seated on a throne, is depicted as a large single round-arched structure, which could represent a castle hall. Its design is based on illustrations depicted in the *Harley Psalter* of the tenth/eleventh century. There is another round-headed pagoda-like building shown during this episode. It is empty and its function and location are not known, but it seems to divide William's messengers into two groups, one of which contains the dwarf ostler, Turold.

The following scenes depict the comings and goings of emissaries between Beaurain and Rouen. Beaurain lies some 160km (100 miles) from Rouen, a considerable distance even for mounted messengers, and the protracted and possibly acrimonious bargaining, shown on the Tapestry, could have taken several weeks to complete. The Tapestry deals with the Ponthieu negotiations at considerable length, providing some impression of the nature of the transactions, the speed with which the messengers travelled and the complicated, perhaps even confused, nature of the discussions between Count Guy and Duke William over the details of Harold's release.

Belrem Castle or Rouen Tower?

Towards the end of the Ponthieu episode, Duke William is shown seated on a throne receiving news from an English messenger. Immediately to his left is a substantial fortified structure whose location has been disputed. It has been argued that this image represents Guy of Ponthieu's motte-and-bailey castle at Beaurain or Belrem as it appears in the Tapestry caption.[5] A large earthwork motte still survives there, forming the remnant of a formidable defensive castle dating from Guy's rule as count (1053–1100).

The size of this monument suggests that Guy was more important than he is often portrayed, but the arguments that claim that Beaurain Castle is the building shown on the Tapestry are not convincing. Taylor suggested that the multicoloured stone structure was an outer defensive circuit – an *enceinte* – and that the two guards, who are looking towards William, are standing in front of a motte with a tower on the top. If Taylor is right, the castle at Beaurain was depicted in more specific detail than the other castles on the Tapestry. Furthermore, it would mean that the castle at Beaurain was the most formidable of all the Tapestry's fortifications. Although the draughtsman who configured the Tapestry may have

The large earthen motte of Beaurain Castle. It seems probable that a fortification was originally built here in response to Viking attacks up the Canche Valley. It could have been constructed here after the abandonment of Quentovic, which lay close to the coast downstream.

Bayeux Tapestry. The Tower at Rouen.

known of this fortification, and perhaps its size was a matter of general knowledge, it is unlikely he would have ever seen it. It is also unlikely that the castle had stone walls around the perimeter; it is much more probable that in the mid-eleventh century it was a purely earth and timber construction.

The Tower at Rouen was undoubtedly built of stone. It had been erected as one of the earliest stone keep castles in northern France, probably on the site of the Carolingian palace, the '*Rotomagensis urbis palatia*'. Robert de Torigni asserts that the new castle was built by William's great-grandfather Duke Richard I in the second half of the tenth century, but recently it has been argued that it dates from the time of Richard II (996–1026).[6] The Haute Vielle Tower at Rouen was built in the south-east angle of the Roman city wall, facing a possible threat from France upriver. This building can be compared to the residence of the Carolingian counts, which traditionally had been at the other end of the town, guarding the approach from the sea.[7] Later property boundaries indicate that its perimeter enclosed an area of 1.5 hectares. It has been argued that the common alignment of the Tower and the transept of Rouen Cathedral reflected a planned symbolism in the layout of the two main buildings of the city; an argument which is reinforced by the relationship between Duke Richard II and his brother Robert, the archbishop of Rouen from 989.[8]

The form of the streets and plots to the south of the castle indicates the former presence of an outer bailey, where the duke's ships possibly departed and landed. An 'Anchors Street' was recorded in the early thirteenth century immediately to the west of the castle, suggesting ducal naval activity, as the mercantile harbour lay to the west of the walled city. In 1027 the chief of the ducal fleet was Rabel de Tancarville, who possessed the donjon at Rouen and various rights in ports

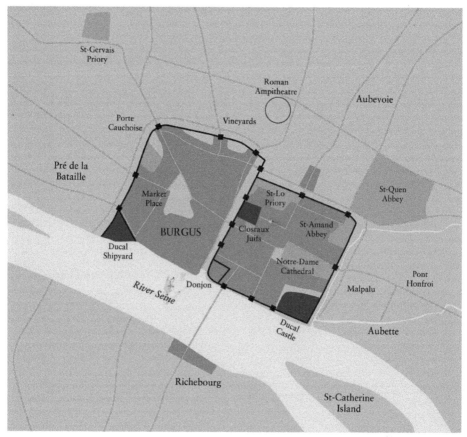

Plan of eleventh century Rouen (after Gauthiez). The Tower depicted on the Tapestry probably occupied the site marked 'Ducal Castle' in the south-east corner of the walled town. The Donjon appears to have occupied an earlier fortified site in the south-west facing possible Viking attacks from downstream. The Ducal shipyard, which undoubtedly played a major role in fitting the invasion fleet, lay in the south-west corner of the Burgus which was added to the city c.1000.

on the lower Seine and in the Pays de Caux. Rouen was a significant town, with a population larger than any English city apart from London, and a bridge across the Seine at the western end of the town is first mentioned in the 1080s.

Rouen Tower was a large quadrilateral-shaped building, whose design seems to have been based on earlier fortified towers at Chartres, Laon and Pithiviers. The tower's size became proverbial among contemporary Normans and, like the later Tower of London, it became known simply as 'the Tower'. It has been suggested that the design of the White Tower (Tower of London), started c.1080, was partly based on the Tower in Rouen.[9] The Tower combined several functions including those of a ducal residence, a military and administrative centre, and a ducal prison. It was adjacent to the ducal palace, which appears on the Tapestry soon afterwards.

There is no surviving description of Rouen Tower, which was destroyed by the French king Philippe Augustus, when he took over Normandy in 1204, but there are references to various parts of its structure. There was a tower chapel dedicated to St Romain, a kitchen, a reception room, ducal quarters, and a gallery linking it to the great hall in the ducal palace. During its lifetime the size of the Rouen Tower became legendary, leading to the twelfth-century expression 'weighing as much as the Tower of Rouen'.[10] Bishop Odo was imprisoned here between 1082 and 1086 for raising a private army in England. It is ironic that the place where Odo spent what must have been a miserable and frustrating four years of his life is portrayed so proudly on the bishop's own greatest lasting creation, the Bayeux Tapestry.

Defensive stone towers of this type had first appeared in France during the later tenth century; some of the best-known examples are those of Château Gontier, Loches and Montrichard in the Loire valley, built by Fulk Nerra, Count of Anjou. In Normandy, the Rouen Tower seems to have been similar in design to the *Turris Famosa* at Ivry-la-Bataille (Eure), which was built c.1000 by Albereda, wife of Rodulf, Count of Bayeux, half-brother of Duke Richard I. According to Orderic Vitalis, Albereda had the architect of the tower, Lanfred, beheaded after the fortress was completed 'so that he should not build another like it elsewhere'. Earlier Lanfred had served as master of works for the construction of the tower at Pithiviers in the Loire Valley. Orderic records that Ivry 'is the famous tower, huge and very strong ... which Hugh, bishop of Bayeux and brother of John, archbishop of Rouen, held against the Dukes of Normandy for a long time'.[11] The surviving tower ruins at Ivry were cleared and investigated during the second half of the twentieth century, when it was found that the base of the early eleventh-century tower measured 25m x 32m. It would seem that the Great Tower at Ivry was slightly earlier than or contemporary with its counterpart in Rouen. Furthermore, although there remain questions about the dating of the early phases of the tower, it is remarkably similar in scale, proportion and layout to the post-Conquest White Tower in London.[12] It is even possible that this form of defensive structure had appeared in England before 1066 and recent analysis of the free-standing St George's Tower, Oxford, indicates a date of c.1050.[13]

Having satisfactorily completed the negotiations for Harold's release, Guy hands Harold over to Duke William. The Tapestry provides no clue as to where the transfer occurred, but William of Poitiers suggests that it was at Eu on the River Bresle, which formed the boundary between Normandy and Ponthieu. It was a location known to William, as it was here that the duke had married his wife, Matilda, the daughter of Baldwin V, Count of Flanders, in around 1050. The ceremony had probably taken place in the chapel of the castle at Eu, which is the only part of the Norman fortification which survives today.

The Tapestry then shows William accompanying Harold, still with his falcon and hunting dogs, back to Rouen. There is a turret, possibly representing one of Rouen's city gates, where a sentry is stationed on the lookout for the duke's return. The duke is next seen seated on a throne, with his English 'guests', within a great hall or palace at Rouen.

This is the 'Tower Hall' at Rouen, recorded in 1074, where the dukes of Normandy used to hold court; its design is distinguished by a row of Romanesque blind semicircular arches along the top of the walls. This technique had earlier been used in the great reception hall at the Abbey of St Trinité (Abbaye Aux Dames) in Caen, which had been founded by William in 1059–60. The hall was clearly of considerable size and can be compared to the extant Hall of the Exchequer built by Henry I for his palace in Caen. Remains of an earlier ducal palace at Caen survived next to the Exchequer until they were destroyed by Allied bombing in 1944. Their footprint has been laid out in concrete on the ground.

Harold has four men with him carrying shields and lances and the group are presumably making plans for the forthcoming Breton campaign. The next scene is one of the Tapestry's great enigmas, which bears the caption, 'Where one cleric and

Bayeux Tapestry. Duke William, seated on a throne meets Earl Harold, probably in the ducal palace in Rouen. In the frieze below there is a naked carpenter planing a plank with an adze; probably an ironic reference to the building of the invasion fleet two years later.

The Exchequer in Caen Castle from an eighteenth century drawing, before the ground was cleared from around the building.

Aelfgyva'. There is a narrow building, supported by two spiral columns topped by carved dragon heads, in which stands a woman (Aelfgyva), whose head is covered, wearing a full-length robe. The cleric, who is portrayed outside the building, is either slapping the woman's face or gesticulating with her. Immediately behind there is another narrow, turreted building, which could represent a church. In the lower border is a nude male figure who mimics the cleric's stance. It may have related to a sexual scandal which had some bearing upon the succession to the English throne, but despite much scholarly speculation the location and meaning of this episode remains a mystery.[14]

Mont-St-Michel

According to the Tapestry, William's army entered Brittany by crossing the estuary of the River Cousenon, which joins the sea at Mont-St-Michel. The island monastery was a sacred location associated with a legendary story involving the Archangel Michael which became an important centre of art, scholarship and pilgrimage from Carolingian times. Historically, the island sanctuary was a site of considerable symbolic importance and over the centuries has been claimed by both Normandy and Brittany, as well as enjoying short periods of independence from both. The abbey was under ducal patronage and since 1048 William had installed a series of Norman abbots. Its prominence on the Tapestry would have

Aerial view of Mont-St-Michel surmounted by the abbey.

Bayeux Tapestry. Earl Harold rescuing Norman soldiers in the quicksand of the estuary of the River Cousenon.

reminded observers that the abbey was effectively now under Norman rule and, as if to confirm this control, William's brother, Robert of Mortain, carried the standard of St Michael during the Battle of Hastings.

Its depiction on the Tapestry may also be a reference to a patron. It has been argued that Abbot Scolland (or Scotland), who was abbot of St Augustine's, Canterbury (1070–87), played an important role in the making of the Tapestry. Before the abbot moved to Canterbury he had been a scribe and treasurer at Mont-St-Michel and the character in the border sitting to the right of the abbey church of Mont-St-Michel, and pointing at it, may actually be Scolland. Another possible link between Mont-St-Michel, Bayeux and Canterbury is that Bishop Odo attracted monks from the island abbey to house his new abbey of St Vigor in Bayeux at about this time.

Mont-St-Michel marks an important transition point in the Tapestry, denoting the onset of hostilities between Duke William and Count Conan of Brittany. The events at Mont-St-Michel also mark a distinct change of pace in the narrative. After the mysterious Aelfgyva episode, Duke William and his men are shown riding sedately towards Mont-St-Michel, but immediately following this Earl Harold is depicted rescuing the Norman soldiers from the quicksand, after which there are hectic scenes of warfare.

Since the eleventh century, as a result of its poorly defined estuarine channel, the River Cousenon has changed its course from one side of Mont-St-Michel to

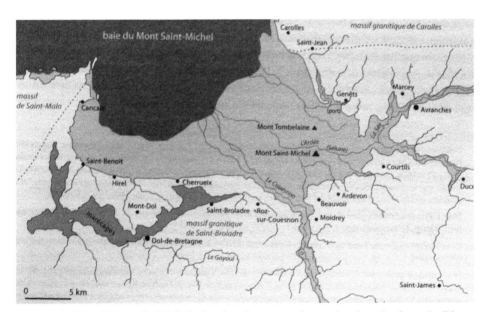

Plan of the Bay of Mont-St-Michel, showing the extent of estuarine deposits from the Rivers Cousenon, Sée and Sélune. Mont-St-Michel and Mont Tombelaine represent granitic outcrops (Bouet and Desbordes, 2005).

the other. The Cousenon estuary is characterized by large quantities of silt and mud and is notorious for its quicksand. The Tapestry provides a graphic image of Norman soldiers and their horses sinking into quicksand. On this occasion Harold is portrayed heroically, as it is he who rescues the soldiers – the caption reads simply, 'Here Duke Harold dragged them from the sand'. Despite the importance of rivers to communication, as boundaries and as barriers at the time, the Cousenon is the only stretch of water to be specifically named on the whole of the Tapestry.

The Bay of Mont-St-Michel is one of the most steeply tidal points in Europe, with a tidal variation of 15m (50ft). The highest spring tides occur after a new moon and a full moon, particularly at the spring and autumn equinoxes. On these occasions the sea surrounds the mount completely, compared to times of the neap tide, when there is no water around the mount even at high tide. Around the time of the spring equinox, the rivers that flow into St-Michel Bay – the Cousenon, the Sélune and the Sée – are subjected to a tidal bore (Mascaret).

This is basically a wave of water which is projected upstream. It is almost a kilometre in width when it starts in the bay and before it divides into the respective river channels. It is just possible that the incident involving Earl Harold rescuing the Norman soldiers coincided with the bore and would have left a deep impression

The tidal bore or Mascaret in the Bay of Mont St Michel during the spring tides. The biggest tide variation in Europe is experienced in the bay, with an average fifteen metre amplitude.

Bayeux Tapestry. Mounted soldiers of William and Harold passing in front of Mont- St-Michel. The pointing hand to the right of the church may be that of Abbot Scolland of St Augustine's, a possible patron of the Tapestry. (See p. 70)

on witnesses. The presence of two fishes in the lower frieze, back to back but connected by some form of cord, has been interpreted by some as an allusion to the zodiacal sign of Pisces, perhaps placing the events in the second half of February or March, roughly corresponding to the time of the spring tides. However, despite the lack of firm evidence, it is generally believed that the Breton campaign took place later in the year of 1064.

In the background to this episode, Mont-St-Michel is named and is shown as a hill with a Romanesque structure on its summit. The small tenth-century Carolingian church here comprised a rectangular nave and square chancel built on the summit of the rock, with a lower sanctuary (the chapel of Notre-Dame-Sous-Terre) on a terrace below. This chapel is the oldest architectural structure on Mont-St-Michel and it was retained in order to support the western section of the Romanesque nave. It appears to have replaced an eighth-century oratory dedicated to the putative founder of the abbey, St Aubert of Avranches (d.720).

The chapel consists of two parallel naves, separated by a thick wall pierced by two arches, and terminated by two small barrel-vaulted shrines. These were probably dedicated to the Archangel Michael and the Virgin Mary. The structure is characteristically Carolingian, with thick walls (up to 2m), roughly cut stone

Romanesque interior of the Benedictine abbey church at Mont-St-Michel dating from the later eleventh century, showing the south wall of the nave.

blocks, and brick arches. There are remains of plaster decoration under the arches of the central wall.

The abbey was rebuilt on a much grander scale around 1023 by William of Volpiano, during the reign of William's grandfather Duke Richard II. The transept crossing of the abbey church was located at the pinnacle of the mount and the remainder of the church had to be supported by building up from the natural rock below. Thus there are numerous rooms including crypts and chapels built into the massive foundations required to support the church.

The Romanesque abbey church was conceived as one of the largest in eleventh-century Normandy, but only four of the original seven bays of the building survive, as the western end of the nave collapsed. Eleventh-century naves in the duchy are characterized by the superimposition of large rounded arches, galleries or false galleries, and tall windows. This high interior elevation was made possible by the use of a wooden ceiling, which not only weighed less than stone vaulting, but also exerted less pressure on the walls. The north side of the nave collapsed twenty years after it was built and was reconstructed in the twelfth century. The eleventh-century arches were built of rubble infill between two facings of dressed stone. The masonry was gradually compressed under the weight and the cross arches of the aisles have correspondingly been distorted. In contrast, the twelfth-century

Reconstruction of Mont-St-Michel in the tenth century by Paul Gout, chief architect of Monuments Historiques (1910)

north wall was built entirely of dressed stone, which has not been compressed. The stones were also slightly tapered, which reduced the lateral thrust and added to the stability of the building.

Some scholars have argued that the designer of the Tapestry was familiar with the detailed construction on Mont-St-Michel as it depicts the church sited on a

Reconstruction of the pre-Romanesque church at Mont-St-Michel (after Lewis). It may have been this building that was depicted on the Tapestry.

platform with artificial supporting structures rising from the rocky promontory on either side.

The nave was not completed until 1085 and it is therefore possible that the Carolingian church was still standing at the time the Tapestry was made, but Lewis argues that neither the new nave nor the earlier church is represented in the Tapestry. On the Tapestry the church appears as a rectangular building with a trapezoid pitched roof – taking the same form as Bosham Church.[15] Two towers which are shown on either side of the church on the Tapestry might actually be buttresses.[16] Lewis claims that here as elsewhere it was contemporary illuminated manuscripts and reliquary shrines and not real buildings which influenced much of the Tapestry's ecclesiastical architecture. Nevertheless, the image of Mont-St-Michel is a striking one and, 'Even if the depiction of the abbey's architecture is not 'authentic', the totality of its presentation is effective in forwarding the aims of the narrative'.[17]

It is significant that the Mont-St-Michel episode is not recorded in any other account and it has been suggested that its presence is linked to the patronage of the Tapestry. The specific reference to the River Cousenon and the roughly accurate depiction of the mount at Mont-St-Michel do suggest that the designer of the Tapestry was familiar with the geography of the area, but was not attempting to produce a precise picture of the church or the local topography. Mont-St-Michel remains a spectacular landmark and is one of the most popular tourist sites in Europe. The mount was designated a World Heritage Site in 1979 and attracts nearly three and a half million visitors a year.[18]

This seated figure appears in the upper border above the scene where Earl Harold is rescuing Norman troops from the quicksand. It is possibly Scolland, abbot of St Augustine's, Canterbury (1070–1089), who had been a monk-scribe at Mont-St-Michel, and who may have played an important role in the creation of the Tapestry.

Chapter 4

Castles and the Breton Campaign

The Breton campaign is a self-contained narrative story within the Tapestry, showing Earl Harold participating in an expedition with Duke William along the north-eastern boundary of Brittany. It could have been included as a deliberate forerunner of the conquest of England, with roughly the same sequence of events – a water crossing, cavalrymen fighting against foot soldiers, followed by the overthrow of the enemy. Or it could have been a commentary on recent political events, for example, how William exerted his influence over Brittany and how the Norman dukes replaced the House of Rennes as the principal patrons of Mont-St-Michel.[1] Brittany is a distinctive geographical region, known as the Armorican Peninsula, characterized by granite uplands, but its eastern boundary has always been poorly defined. The Breton Marches consisted of undulating, heavily wooded countryside with a network of small rivers and streams. Historically it shared its geographical character with its neighbours – Normandy to the north-east, Maine and Anjou to the east and Poitou to the south. William's acquisition of Maine in 1063 would have increased the Normans' involvement in the affairs of the Breton border. In particular, the Breton capital, Rennes, lay only 40km (26 miles) to the west of Maine and would have been of considerable political interest to the duke.

This section of the Tapestry includes the unique depiction of a group of Breton border castles at Dol, Rennes and Dinan. In addition to the three Breton mottes, another is shown later at Bayeux and also one in the course of construction at Hastings, after William's invasion fleet has landed in England. The Tapestry castles all appear to have had an earthen motte capped by a wooden tower, but they differ significantly in detail. The depiction of this episode is also unusual as the designer appears to exhibit some knowledge of the region in which the Breton campaign takes place.

Information about the Breton campaign is sparse and there are no reliable Breton sources, but the outline story, provided largely by William of Poitiers, is that in 1064 Duke Conan II of Brittany was engaged in operations against rebels along the border with Normandy. Some of the rebels, notably Conan's vassal Riwallon 1 of Dol, appealed to William of Normandy for help and the duke, accompanied by Earl Harold and his contingent of Englishmen, invaded Brittany. Riwallon was being besieged in Dol by Conan and William was able to relieve him after the town fell to a Norman assault. Conan retreated towards Rennes where he met up with

Geoffrey of Anjou. At this stage, according to the records, William then retired back to Normandy at the end of an inconclusive campaign. Riwallon was exiled and the border towns returned into the hands of Duke Conan.

Some chroniclers, such as William of Jumièges, do not even mention the campaign, while others including Orderic Vitalis dismiss it summarily. Its prominence on the Tapestry served to demonstrate William's prowess as a military leader and to confirm the relationship between William and Harold as that of lord and vassal. The designer of the Tapestry may have adapted events earlier in William's reign as duke, when he successfully besieged Norman border towns. Or, it could have been recalling William's success in conquering the province of Maine in 1063, when he besieged and captured strongholds such as Mayenne and Le Mans, transposing those victories on to the strategic towns within the Breton Marches.

The Tapestry tells a more heroic story than the chroniclers, during which William is shown as a forceful and successful campaigner, chasing Conan to Dol, Rennes and finally to Dinan, where he captures the town. The whole of the Breton campaign, which provides a military prelude to the Battle of Hastings, is as spectacular as it is unbelievable, despite the detail that is shown on the Tapestry.

After William's army has passed Mont-St-Michel they attack Dol, where Count Conan is seen escaping from the burning wooden tower, on top of the castle motte, by way of an improbably stiff rope. The Norman knights are then pictured riding past the castle at Rennes without attacking it and then besieging the castle at Dinan. Conan is shown surrendering the castle here by passing a set of large keys to the besiegers.

Bayeux Tapestry. The castle at Dol Castle is first of the Breton mottes to be depicted; in this scene Count Conan is seen escaping from a burning tower by way of a rope. A wooden bridge with steps leads to the base of the tower on top of the motte.

Bayeux Tapestry. Cavalrymen riding past the castle at Rennes, shown here with steps leading to a wooden palisade on top of the motte. The mound seems to be covered with hides or possibly shields.

At this point the Tapestry's account of the campaign comes to an end with a scene showing William giving arms to Harold. This appears to have been a Norman ceremony that had been adopted by Edward the Confessor in England. It took the form of bestowing a coat of chain mail to the recipient, the placing of a helmet on the head and the presentation of a 'belt of knighthood'. The precise implications of the ceremony within the context of the Tapestry are disputed by scholars. Some argue that it was recognition of Harold's military valour during the

Bayeux Tapestry. Dinan is the third of the Breton castles on the Tapestry. It has a bridge crossing the motte ditch. Soldiers are trying to burn the motte palisade, while Conan is passing the castle keys to one of the besiegers.

Bayeux Tapestry. In this symbolic scene Duke William is giving arms to Earl Harold, either to reward him for his part in the Breton campaign or to establish that the earl is William's vassal.

Breton campaign, while others believe that Harold was submitting himself to his lord and recognizing William's eventual right to become king of England.

William of Poitiers places this episode before the Breton campaign, claiming that the duke 'gave him [Harold] and his companions arms and elite horses' before leading them into combat. The Tapestry places the arms-giving adjacent to the oath-swearing scene. This may have been to heighten the drama of Harold's oath by demonstrating the earl's subservience to William immediately before taking a sacred oath swearing his allegiance to the duke.

The Development of the Castle

As the Carolingian empire divided into semi-autonomous counties and duchies in the tenth century there was a need for private defensive structures against both internal and external threats. Castles evolved at the same time as feudalism and they acquired a symbolic status as a mark of lordship. In the late tenth and early eleventh centuries, Brittany, like Normandy, was moving towards a form of feudalism in which local lords assumed territorial power from the count or duke. One consequence of this development was the building of castles as the seat of their *capita* (estates). Normally, these were constructed with the consent of the ruler, but sometimes without such sanction. Such fortifications were used to maintain the peace, but could also form bases for rebellion against the central authority.

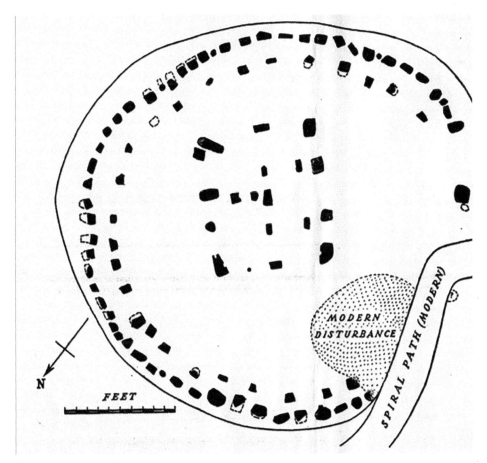

Abinger, Surrey. The classic plan of the excavated top of the motte showing postholes for the palisade and for the tower; the latter are believed to extend down to the original ground surface (after Hope-Taylor).

In the first instance, castles seem to have been in the form of simple earthwork enclosures consisting of a bank with a palisade and with an outside ditch. Such fortified enclosures, known as ringworks, would often have been no more than a hectare in size and were usually oval or circular in shape. Within the enclosure there would have been a hall and a chapel together with other ancillary buildings. There have been excavations of such structures in England at Goltho (Lincs.) and Sulgrave (Northants.). The weakest part of a ringwork defence was the entrance, and wooden towers were built to act as gatehouses. These gatehouses were particularly susceptible to burning and one plausible explanation for the development of the motte was that earth was piled up around the base of the tower in order to protect it. It has been demonstrated at Abinger (Surrey) that a wooden structure was built first and then the motte built up around it. Such a construction would have been far more stable than a tower erected on top of a recently built mound, where fear of subsidence would have been a constant concern. The lower stage of the tower on top of the motte was open, as shown at the castle at Dinan on the Tapestry. The excavator, Brian Hope-Taylor, called it 'a sort of box on stilts'.

This design of a tower is depicted on a carving from Westminster Hall, in which a man is shown chopping at one of the supporting pillars (see p. 88). There is also evidence from a motte in Denmark where the supporting stilts of a wooden tower rested on stone pads on the old ground surface at the base of the motte.[2] At South Mimms (Hertfordshire), a timber tower encased in a motte also had its foundations on the natural ground level. This castle dates from about 1140 as does that at Farnham (Surrey), where a stone tower of similar date was sitting at ground level and was also encased within an earthen mound.[3] These and other examples suggest that the tower and motte were normally built at the same time, i.e. conjointly. This technique was also used for incorporating a well within the motte that had its head near the top of the mound. At Oxford Castle a large earthen motte incorporates a well-chamber just below its summit.

One of the earliest references to a castle comes in 843 when the Vikings were raiding the 'townships and fortified sites of the districts of Mauges, Tiffauges and the Pays de Rays', when Bego, Duke of Aquitaine had built 'on the banks of the Loire recently not far from the city of Nantes a castle (*castellum*) on which he had bestowed his own name'. The *castrum* Begonis has been identified as the motte at Bougon (Loire-Atlantique), which was destroyed by the extension of Nantes airport in the 1970s.[4]

Other castles were built by the barons in Anjou during the late tenth and early eleventh centuries, in particular by Fulk III and his son, Geoffrey II, who gained reputations as prolific castle builders. From Anjou, they spread into Normandy and Brittany and then other parts of Europe. Duke William was well aware of the threat that was posed by such fortifications to centralized control and introduced laws to prohibit the building of fortifications over a certain size without his express permission. The duke's *Consuetudines et Justicie* legally defined the permissible size of ditches, banks and palisades. He also insisted on garrisoning troops of his own men within baronial castles in Normandy.

The Motte and Bailey

Mottes were man-made earthen mounds, often of considerable size, with towers on top of them; initially they were built of timber, as shown on the Tapestry, but they were often later replaced by stone structures. Attached to the mounds there were usually enclosed courtyards or baileys, surrounded by a protective palisade and ditch. Motte castles and motte-and-bailey castles acted as garrison forts during offensive military operations, as strongholds, and in many cases as aristocratic residences and the centre of local or royal administration. Such structures could be built rapidly and, if destroyed, easily replaced. Together with ringworks these were the forms of the first castles thrown up in England during the early phases of the Norman conquest of England. Such castles were built in towns, villages and open countryside and generally occupied strategic positions dominating their immediate locality and, as a result, are the most visually impressive monuments of the early post-Conquest period surviving in the British landscape today. As such they are particularly important for the study of Norman Britain and of the imposition of Norman rule in England and Wales.

The motte may have appeared at about the same time as free-standing defensive towers were becoming common in the tenth/eleventh centuries. Both mottes and fortified towers became known as donjons as they fulfilled the same role and had the same symbolic importance. They formed the military strongpoint of the castle

The motte at Tonbridge Castle, built immediately after the Conquest by Richard fitz Gilbert to guard the Medway crossing.

and, in many cases, the lord's residence. Although many were occupied for only a short period of time, motte castles continued to be built and occupied from the eleventh to the thirteenth centuries, after which they tended to be abandoned or superseded by other forms of defensive structure.

The term 'motte and bailey' is used to describe the earth and timber castles of the Norman era. Both 'motte' (Old French, meaning mound) and 'bailey' (Old French, meaning enclosure) were in use in the eleventh century, but their combination to describe a type of castle is a piece of modern archaeological categorization. There are over 600 motte or motte-and-bailey castles in Britain, with examples known from most regions. Substantial mottes dating from this period can still be seen at places such as Windsor, Wallingford and Oxford. A large motte was also built at Canterbury within a few years of the Conquest and it is possible that the earthen mounds depicted on the Tapestry were based on the castle, known as Dane John which would have been visible, not very far away from St Augustine's.

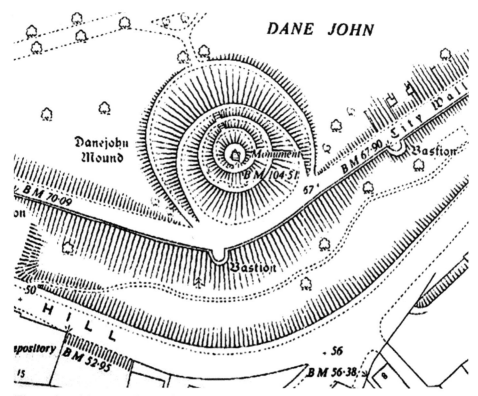

DANE JOHN

The earthwork known as Dane John, sits in the southern part of the walled town of Canterbury, and was originally a Romano–British burial mound. Soon after the conquest it was converted into a motte, but was replaced by the stone keep of Canterbury Castle in the 1120's. Significantly the motte would have been visible from St Augustine's at the time the Tapestry was being made. The name appears to be a corruption of the Norman-French *donjon*. (fortification)

Distribution of earthwork castles in north-west France in 1965. The coverage for Brittany, in particular, has been much expanded by more recent regional studies (after Soyer, J., *Annales de Normandie* 15, 1965).

The reconstruction of an eleventh-century motte and bailey castle at Saint-Sylvain-d'Anjou (Maine-et-Loire).

There are large numbers of Motte castles in Brittany and Anjou, as well as a significant number in Normandy. Mottes are also found in the Low Countries and Sicily.

An early reference to a motte castle dates from 1026 when Count Eudes of Blois raised 'a timber tower of marvellous height upon the motte' at La Motte-Montboyau, near Tours. In 1060 it is recorded that Arnulf II, seneschal of Count Eustace of Boulogne, raised 'a very high motte or donjon' at Ardres (Pas-de-Calais). The author of this account may be as guilty of embellishment as the designer of the Tapestry was when portraying his extravagant motte towers. He then built a 'great and lofty house' upon the motte. This was of three storeys with cellars, storerooms and granaries on the ground floor; residential apartments, including the great chamber, the kitchens, and a privy chamber with a fire on the second floor; and other small chambers for sons and daughters on the third.[5]

Another account, dating from around 1130, describes a motte at 'Merchem' (possibly Merkem, near Dixmude, Belgium):

> There was near the atrium of the church, a fortress (*munitio*), which we may call castle (*castrum*) or municipium, exceedingly high, built after the custom of that land by the lord many years before. For it is the habit of the magnates and nobles of those parts, who spend most of their time fighting and slaughtering their enemies, in order thus to be safer from their opponents and with greater power to vanquish their equals and suppress their inferiors, to raise a mound (*agger*) of earth as high as they can and dig a ditch about it as wide and deep as possible. The space on top of the mound is enclosed by a palisade of very strong hewn logs, strengthened at intervals with as many towers as their means can provide. In the middle of the space within the palisade they build a residence (*domus*), or, dominating everything, a keep (*arx*). The entrance to the fortress is by means of a bridge, which rising from the outer side of the moat and supported by double or even triple columns at suitable intervals as it ascends, reaches to the top of the mound.[6]

At Durham Castle, contemporaries provide a description of how the motte-and-bailey superstructure arose from the 'tumult of rising earth' with a keep extending 'into thin air, strong within and without' with a 'stalwart house … glittering with beauty in every part',[7] a description which could equally apply to the flamboyant motte towers on the Tapestry.

Relatively few mottes have been systematically excavated to test the raised tower interpretation. One much quoted example is that of Abinger, Surrey, where excavations found four substantial postholes on the top of the motte, which appeared to extend down to the original ground level. Reconstructions of Abinger Castle show these posts supporting a raised tower. An excavated site in Normandy, at Grimbosq, appears to have had a similar design. This motte lies at the heart

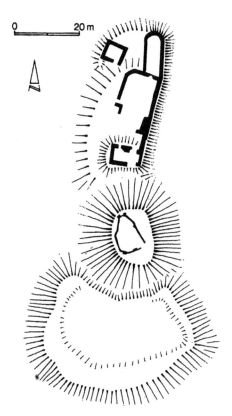

Plan of the motte d'Olivet at Grimbosq in Lower Normandy, 15 km. south of Caen (Decaens, J., *Archéologie Medievale* 11, 1981). It was excavated in the 1970s when a large hall, chapel and kitchen were found as well as a forge and stables. It appears to have been built by Raoul Cinglais Angevins, an ancestor of the Taison family, who arrived in Normandy between 1017 and 1025.

of the forest of Grimbosq, part of Cinglais, a small Basse-Normandie region located some 15km to the south of Caen, squeezed between the River Orne and its tributary the Laize. The site, which was excavated between 1975 and 1978, was built by Cinglais of Raoul l'Angevin, ancestor of the Taisson family, who arrived in Normandy between 1017 and 1025. The very short existence of the motte of Grimbosq, before the middle of the eleventh century, should be placed within the context of rivalries between two branches of the Taisson family, at a time when ducal authority was in decline; Raoul Taisson being one of the conspirators who was later defeated by William at the Battle of Val-ès-Dunes in 1047.

The castle is built on a rocky spur formed at the junction of two valleys with steep flanks that afforded it good natural defence. The motte, on which rose a wooden tower and observation or lookout post, occupies a central position. It is surrounded by two courtyards. The north one is narrower and occupies the end of the spur. The excavations revealed the residence of the seigneur, a chapel and a kitchen. There was also a small masonry tower that gave access to a walkway, allowing the top of the motte to be reached. The larger south courtyard appears to have been a horse enclosure. The remains of a forge and a probable stable were also uncovered, and the recovery of numerous horseshoes and pieces of harness seems to confirm this interpretation.

Other archaeological evidence for mottes in pre-Conquest Normandy is rare, but there is evidence for mottes in parts of southern Italy and Sicily conquered by the Normans. Elsewhere in France, at Doué-la-Fontaine (Anjou), an unfortified, stone ground-floor hall of around 900 was converted into a two-storey defensible building with first-floor entry added later in the same century. In the eleventh century this building was 'enmotted', that is, a mound was piled around its base.[8] Over the past thirty years a large number of mottes have been identified in Brittany and many of these would have originated in the unsettled conditions of the tenth and eleventh centuries. In a survey of the department of Finistère alone some 166 mottes were identified[9] and work in other parts of Brittany has produced comparable results. The indicative place name 'motte' is particularly common in the border region with Normandy, where large numbers of feudal fortifications might be anticipated. Excavations at several mottes in Brittany have shown that there was a tendency for the original wooden defences to be replaced by stone structures. At Leskelen en Plabennec in Finistère, the motte is a stone-revetted structure ringed by a deep ditch. In the eleventh century, a large house of wood and clay, roofed with thatch, was constructed and defended by a wooden palisade. The motte reached its final form c.1100, when stone ramparts were built on its summit, the wooden house by then having been replaced by a stone tower.[10] A similar pattern has been identified at nearby Lamber en Ploumoguer, where a stone tower lay on top of a layer of burnt material containing coins of Conan II (1040–66), which has been interpreted as evidence of an earlier wooden structure.[11]

The Tapestry Castles

Considerable attention has rightly been paid by archaeologists and historians to the five castles depicted on the Tapestry. These are undoubtedly the earliest surviving visual record of castle mottes, but how realistic are they and how much do they tell us about such eleventh-century fortifications? Interpretations on the veracity of the depictions of castles have changed radically in recent years. Musset's opinion that despite some limitations 'the Tapestry's images of castles retain enormous importance for archaeologists, far more detailed than other surviving images'[12] was one which was commonly held throughout the twentieth century. In the last few years scholars have viewed the castle representations far more critically, an approach which is expressed at its most extreme by Woodman, 'None of these places in reality ever looked remotely like their depiction on the Tapestry'.[13]

The defensive elements of these fortifications take various forms. Dol is shown as a square tower with rounded battlements; Rennes has square battlements on top of a wooden palisade. Bayeux seems to have a battlement palisade, perhaps constructed of wood. Likewise, Dinan seems to have a wooden palisade, composed of V-shaped elements. Hastings Castle does not have battlements, but is fortified by a rounded palisade of wood. Battlements associated with forts and city walls are common in other contemporary illustrations. The defensive mounds depicted on the Tapestry differ in detail; Dinan's mound is rounded, with a ditch on either side, while Dol also has a surrounding ditch, but the mound itself is steeper, with a flatter summit. A similar flat-topped hill also serves Rennes, but here the ditch has a square form, with a pronounced defensive structure – perhaps an outer wall or palisade. In contrast Bayeux and Hastings castles do not have defensive ditches. Whilst Bayeux rises from a large and steep motte, Hastings Castle sits on a neatly rounded, quite shallow mound. The only other building shown occupying a hill is the abbey of Mont-St-Michel, which sits on a natural island mound.

The depiction of the four French sites as mottes provides interesting detail about this type of castle, but also evidence for the debate about motte origins. The four illustrations give a broadly similar impression: of a mound surmounted by a wooden palisaded building reached via a bridge. Upright members are shown in the palisades at Rennes and Dinan, as well as in the superstructure of the building at Bayeux. At Dinan the building has a convex roofline, a feature which is the result of the bow-sided plan common in many early medieval timber houses. Dol is less obviously a timber site, and here and at Bayeux the internal evidence could easily be interpreted as a mixture of timber and stone. At Dol a tower (*turris*), probably of stone, was mentioned in the mid-twelfth century.

The value of the depictions must be judged from general considerations rather than from direct comparison with the places concerned. The fact that each one is different in character might give the impression that the Tapestry's designer was familiar with each of the fortifications, but although the differences might reflect actual variations in the construction of mottes, there is no evidence that they are accurate representations of what was on the ground. It is now generally agreed that the designer represented the castles schematically, with perhaps some elements of authenticity.

Another consideration should be borne in mind when viewing the Breton castles on the Tapestry and that is that the designer was simply using castles as shorthand to portray whole towns. Certainly, the defensive circuits of some towns in the region would have occupied no more than that of an extended outer bailey in the eleventh century. For example, the enceinte at Dinan only occupied 8 or 9 hectares until 1421, after which the whole town, an area of 100 hectares, was enclosed by walls.[14]

Dol

Dol, the first of the Breton marcher castles depicted on the Tapestry, was a site associated with early Christianity in Brittany; a Benedictine monastery was reputedly founded here by St Samson in AD 548. The Romanesque cathedral here was destroyed in 1203, but on the Grande Rue of Dol there survive some fine twelfth-century stone houses, most notably, the arcaded Les Petits Palets.

The Maison des Petits Palets in the Grande Rue des Stuarts, Dol is a remarkable surviving example of domestic Romanesque architecture dating from the twelfth century.

The depiction of Dol Castle is somewhat enigmatic. It is shown in the form of a motte with the profile of a ditch on either side. The tower on top of the mound appears to be triangular in shape, but this was probably an attempt by the designer to create a three-dimensional impression of a square structure. The tower has two storeys; the lower part may have been open to allow circulation of men and horses, while the upper section, which is roofed with crenellations and what appear to be window openings, must have been the living area. The upper part of the tower is decorated with squares, which could have been coloured wooden shingles or just purely imaginative ornamentation. It has also been suggested that these squares might represent protective hides or plates of metal, for which there is some documentary evidence.[15] References to the hanging of shields as a form of fortification defence occur in antiquity and throughout the early Middle Ages.

There are coloured flames coming from the left of the tower, which would in part explain Conan's hurried emergency exit from the building. According to William of Poitiers, Conan was outside the town and not in the castle when the Normans arrived and so his dramatic exit as shown on the Tapestry may be attributed to

Bayeux Tapestry. Wooden tower on the summit of the motte at Dol. On the left are flames and on the right Count Conan is seen escaping by means of a rope.

No trace of the motte depicted on the Tapestry survives at Dol, but there is a fine stretch of medieval wall with bastions on the north-eastern side of the town.

artistic licence. The use of fire against besieged strongholds was common in the early Middle Ages and was one of William the Conqueror's favoured tools of war. Later in the Tapestry, Norman soldiers are setting fire to a house in Hastings, and we know that large areas of northern England were deliberately destroyed by burning during the Harrying of the North in the late 1060s. When William's son Duke Robert Curthose attacked Brionne in the early summer of 1090, it is recorded that, after cutting off the castle from relief forces or supplies, he had arrows with heated metal tips fired into the dry shingle roof of the fortification. The castle caught fire and the defenders were forced to surrender.[16]

There is a substantial wooden bridge shown running from outside the motte ditch at Dol to the summit of the mound and mounted horsemen are beginning to ride across it. Evidence of such a bridge has been found in excavations at Hen Domen (Powys).[17] A pair of fighting birds are shown in front of the motte and can be compared with the two animals shown similarly placed at Rennes Castle. These appear to be purely decorative and are taken from the same bestiary as those portrayed elsewhere in the Tapestry borders.

There are no visible remains of a motte-and-bailey castle at Dol. The old town has a fine set of thirteenth-century defensive stone walls and the location of the castle can be identified at the southern end of the early town. It has been speculated that in 1064 the castle in Dol would already have been built at least partly in stone.[18] In 1076 there was an unsuccessful forty-day siege of Dol Castle, suggesting that

The Porte Mordelaise, Rennes, the main gateway into the medieval city, dating from the thirteenth century. No trace of a motte survives here.

Flat-topped motte at Lesquellen à Plabennec. Excavations here found the lower part of the mound was riveted with flat stones.

the tower was already built of stone by that date; however, a century later, in 1173, Ralph de Fougères and rebels fighting against Henry II believed that the castle at Dol was inadequate for defence against the king's forces and chose to fight in the field instead.[19] At about the same time, Robert of Torigny described Dol Castle as 'the Tower', in the same way that the fortification at Rouen was always known simply as 'the Tower', which might indicate that it was stone-built.

Rennes

There is no other historical record of Rennes Castle featuring in William's Breton campaign. The town lies some 50km to the south of Dol and was sited well away from the known theatre of the campaign. William of Poitiers does mention that, after being ousted from Dol, Conan retreated towards Rennes where he met up with Geoffrey of Anjou, but the Tapestry's inclusion of Rennes within the Breton campaign may well be fictional.

According to the Tapestry, the castle at Rennes was a simpler construction than that at Dol. The motte has walls or palisades around its base and, instead of a flying bridge, there are steps ascending to its summit. It has been suggested that the structure around the base of the mound might represent a dry stone revetment of the type excavated at Heskelen en Plabennec in Finistère, Brittany.[20] Although several commentators have observed that the Tapestry shows William's forces riding past Rennes, in fact it depicts the leading horsemen beginning to cross to the summit of the mound, apparently entering Rennes Castle without any evidence of opposition. The motte has a covering of what look like wooden shingles, but which could also have been hides, shields or stones. It has also been suggested that the sides of the motte are covered with vegetation on which animals are grazing. There is a crenellated palisade around the top of the motte, within which there sits a slender tower. The tower has what appear to be three pilaster strips leading to a conical roof, which might suggest that it was already built of stone. There are two rounded windows shown beneath the roofline.

Historians have argued that the mid-eleventh-century castle at Rennes was likely to have been built at least in part of stone. The Breton historian La Borderie interpreted the Tapestry castle as a 'hexagonal donjon, with an elegant cupola', the upper part being sheathed in lead plates. This interpretation, long out of fashion, is now accepted as a distinct possibility.[21] No evidence of a medieval castle survives

Romanesque capital from Westminster depicting a raised wooden tower, similar in design to the motte tower at Dinan on the Bayeux Tapestry.

at Rennes, although the remains of an inner enceinte within the medieval walled city can be traced at its western end. This is probably where the eleventh-century castle was located.

Dinan

The third of the Breton castles pictured on the Tapestry is at Dinan, which lies 30km (19 miles) to the west of Dol. As with the other locations showing mottes on the Tapestry, no evidence of an early castle survives. The site of the eleventh-century motte is occupied by a stone keep. On the Tapestry there is a large conical motte, with profiled ditches and counterscarps on either side. The structures on the mound are more elaborate than those shown at Dol or Rennes, and consist of a breastwork or bridgehead, palisade and tower. The palisade has a wave-like, decorated top to it and alternating light and dark vertical bands, which indicates that it was probably built of wood. The tower is apparently raised on pillars or stilts, giving room for circulation below, as at Dol. This impression is given credence because the arm of one of the castle defenders appears to pass behind a supporting pillar. This building has been compared with that on an eleventh-century carved capital from Westminster, which shows a crenellated structure raised on four uprights and reached by a sloping bridge or flight of steps.

The capital has been described as follows, 'The heads of two defenders appear between the crenellations. On the left is a kneeling soldier in a short tunic, an axe in one hand and a round shield in the other ... . In front of the soldier steps lead up to the castle gate which swings back behind a third defender whose long sword pierces the attacker's shield and enters his mouth. This explains his kneeling, collapsing position.'[22] This capital is generally regarded as the only contemporary illustration of a timber motte tower apart from those on the Tapestry, but it should be added that the capital does not actually portray a motte.

The upper part of the depiction of the Dinan motte is elaborately decorated and looks rather similar in design to the reliquaries on which Harold swears his oath. The shield-like decoration on the outside could again represent hides or metal placed there for protection. The bridge runs from outside the left-hand ditch and bank, with a gatehouse on the outside this time, across an open ditch to a stepped structure, with a small window, attached to the palisade. Rebel Breton soldiers are attempting to repel the Norman cavalry riders, who appear to be commencing their ascent of the bridge. This image is matched on the other side by the palisade on which Conan stands, passing the keys of the castle to another mounted Norman soldier, who might be Duke William. In front of the castle, two Norman soldiers in full chain-mail armour have dropped their shields and are attempting to set fire to the palisade.

The defensive stone walls of Dinan were admired by the twelfth-century Muslim geographer Idris and it is possible that they were already widely known by the middle of the eleventh century.[23] In the absence of any collaborative historical

Donjon de la duchesse Anne dates from the fourteenth century and forms parts of the medieval ramparts surrounding the old town of Dinan.

evidence it seems unlikely that this particular siege ever took place and that it might have been intended as a warning of what William could and would later achieve in England.

Bayeux

The last of the French castles to appear on the Tapestry was at Bayeux; possibly its appearance is related to Bishop Odo's sponsorship of the hanging. Immediately after the Dinan episode, William presents Harold with arms and the army moves to the ducal castle at Bayeux; the text simply reads, 'Here William came to Bayeux.' The castle is shown with a thin, steep-sided, stepped motte with wavy alternating light and dark bands, perhaps indicating the strata which made up the mound, as seen more graphically portrayed at Hastings Castle. The outer palisade has two towers which sit on the upper steps of the motte on either side of the central domed tower. These towers have windows and are elaborately crenellated, compared to simple outline crenellations seen in the central part of the palisade. The central tower is capped by a cupola roof and a central projecting plain pinnacle, both of which intrude into the Tapestry's upper border. If the roof is domed, this can hardly have been a timber construction. There are no ditches or ramparts shown outside the mound, but a stepped flying bridge projects from the 'cobbled' surface on the left of the castle up to an elaborate gatehouse at the top of the bridge, which is attached to the palisade. The gatehouse has a large window and is fronted by a column with a dragon-head capital. The entrance is more elaborate than those at Dol or Dinan and its large doorway and overall scale are similar to the fore-buildings of later stone keeps. The whole image is neat and taut. There is no evidence of a garrison, but William's approaching troops seem to be about to cross the bridge into the castle.

The depiction of Bayeux Castle differs from the Breton mottes as there is no evidence of a surrounding embankment or protective wall. It appears to be similar in appearance to Farnham in Surrey and South Mimms (Herts.).[24]

Bayeux Castle was located in the north-east corner of the Roman town, whose defences were still standing in the eleventh century. Duke Richard I is known to have built the Tower at Rouen in the second half of the tenth century and there is a reference to him building a fortified palace at Bayeux.[25] Its ornamentation suggests it is more than simply a defensive feature and reminds us that eleventh-century castles were products of domestic as well as of military architecture.

Of all the Tapestry motte depictions, Bayeux is certainly the grandest, perhaps incorporating a high degree of symbolism. Since Bayeux is the site of the Tapestry's central event, Harold's oath, the designer probably exercised considerable licence here and produced a grand, flamboyant structure as a suitable backdrop for this episode.

There are later references to the castle at Bayeux; for instance, in 1164–67 Roger Mowbray went to Normandy in order to defend his title to the castle, which

Bayeux Tapestry. Duke William approaching Bayeux Castle on horseback. On the right the duke is watching Harold swear an oath.

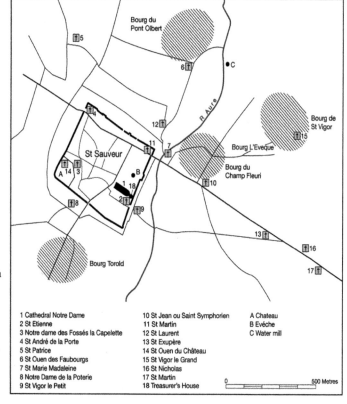

Plan of Medieval Bayeux. In the eleventh century the city was still contained within the boundary of the Roman walls. The castle occupied the western corner of the defences.

1 Cathedral Notre Dame	10 St Jean ou Saint Symphorien	A Chateau
2 St Etienne	11 St Martin	B Evéche
3 Notre dame des Fossés la Capelette	12 St Laurent	C Water mill
4 St André de la Porte	13 St Exupère	
5 St Patrice	14 St Ouen du Château	
6 St Ouen des Faubourgs	15 St Vigor le Grand	
7 St Marie Madaleine	16 St Nicholas	
8 Notre Dame de la Poterie	17 St Martin	
9 St Vigor le Petit	18 Treasurer's House	

Site of the medieval castle at Bayeux, which was destroyed in the eighteenth century and is now a public park.

he claimed had been given to him by King Stephen. Works on the palisade are recorded in 1180. Bayeux Castle also featured in the final expulsion of the English from northern France (with the exception of Calais) in 1450, when castle and city were subjected to assault by cannon for over a fortnight.[26] The castle reputedly with its ten square towers was demolished in 1773. The castle site is today an open public park within the western circuit of the old town walls.

Hastings

It is generally believed that Duke William introduced the castle to England, although a few mottes were built in the Welsh Marches by Normans who accompanied Edward the Confessor when he returned to England in 1051. The Normans used the castle to subdue and then rule the country in the decades after the Conquest. Orderic Vitalis observed that 'the fortifications called castles by the Normans were scarcely known in the English provinces, and so the English – in spite of their courage and love of fighting – could put up only a weak defence to their enemies'.

Although accounts of the Norman invasion record a castle being erected at Pevensey soon after the Normans landed in England, this is not portrayed, and Hastings is the last castle and the only English example depicted in the Tapestry. If 'Hastings' was being used to cover a region in this context, rather than the specific port, it is conceivable that the Tapestry castle was in reality erected at Pevensey.

Bayeux Tapestry. The building of Hastings Castle; the horizontal coloured bands on the motte have been interpreted as the layers of soil which make up the mound. The figure holding the banner and directing operations may be Robert of Mortain or Robert of Eu.

William of Jumièges reports that soon after landing at Pevensey 'with others he [William] hurried to Hastings where he erected another similar fortress'. On the Tapestry, an officer wearing a cloak and holding a banner orders a team of labourers to build a castle at Hastings. To the right of the 'fighting' men, Robert of Mortain or Robert of Eu is standing, holding a banner and directing the operations. Two other men are obeying the officer and are on the way to join a group of five men already at work with shovels and a pick. The workmen's shovels are of wood with a band of metal shown around the digging edge. As metal was expensive and in relatively scarce supply, it would not have been used for the entire shovel blade. Metal strips of the type shown in the Tapestry have been found on many medieval sites in England. The shovels seem to be English in design as they have a hole at the top of the shaft, creating an open handle to make the tool easier to hold. Such handles are not found on contemporary French or Scandinavian equivalents.[27]

Immediately to the left of Hastings Castle are two men apparently fighting with each other, using spades. Commentators argue that this scene was based on a misreading of defence-building soldiers found on Trajan's Column. Possibly, representations of figures on the column were brought back as sketches by Abbot Scolland when he went to Rome to obtain the pope's permission to rebuild St Augustine's Abbey church, sometime before 1073.[28]

The top of the motte is shown with five horizontal bands of different colours. It has been argued that these bands represent layers of earth deposited as the mound was being built. It is possible that each layer was trodden down, perhaps with a clay capping to solidify it. Certainly, the bands do have the appearance of a cross section of an artificially created mound.

The excavation of some mottes has revealed a similar horizontal stratigraphy. At Okehampton (Devon), for instance, the upper part of one end of the motte was laid in this way in preparation for a building to be erected. At Baile Hill, York, clay layers containing turves were laid horizontally at the base of the motte. At Carisbrooke, Isle of Wight, a bedding of stones carried alternating layers of loose and rammed chalk. At Norwich (Norfolk), excavation of an extension of the motte revealed a similar pattern of loam and chalk deposits on top of the old ground surface. Excavation has also revealed consolidating layers on motte surfaces, as at Oxford and Urr (Kirkcudbrightshire) where there were clay cappings, which would have helped limit the extent of erosion on new or enlarged mottes.[29]

On the summit of the mound there is a palisade, which disappears under the upper border. It seems to be constructed of vertical boards, as already seen at Rennes and Dinan, but unlike those on the Breton castles the uprights are not coloured, suggesting that the palisade was not yet complete. The absence of a tower on the top of the Hastings motte also strongly implies that this is work in progress.

The Norman poet Wace (who was a canon of Bayeux at some time and may well have seen the Tapestry) thought this castle had been brought prefabricated from Normandy. His account of the carpenters trimming and drilling the timbers, though not shown on the Tapestry, is consistent with the details of the scenes depicting shipbuilding prior to the invasion. Wace also describes William's invasion fleet offloading sections of a prefabricated castle from the ship of Robert, Count of Eu. At the motte-and-bailey site of Hen Domen in Powys, prefabricated, reused timber sections, complete with bridge and fighting platform, dating from the 1070s were found.[30] It is known that William had made use of prefabricated wooden siege towers since the early 1050s.

If the castle at Hastings was prefabricated, then the piling of a mound around a structure standing directly on the ground surface is exactly what we would expect. It was perhaps why the castle was 'dug' at Hastings: in a sense its timber structure already existed. The only problem with this interpretation is that the obvious thing to bury in a motte would be a tower, whereas this is not what the Tapestry seems to show. Neither did the excavation of the site illuminate the matter. The Norman motte, constructed largely of sand, was buried in a fourteenth-century enlargement and its summit had suffered much destruction. No traces of timberwork were identified and no obvious pattern of stratigraphy observed, the mound consisting of dumps of unstable sand.

It has been suggested that what the workmen are throwing up are bags of sand which were then consolidated with layers of turf represented by the horizontal bands of colour. This might be one way of reconciling the nature of the site with the depiction. In addition, although the argument about the pre-Conquest origin of the church adjacent to the motte may suggest the excavated motte is the same

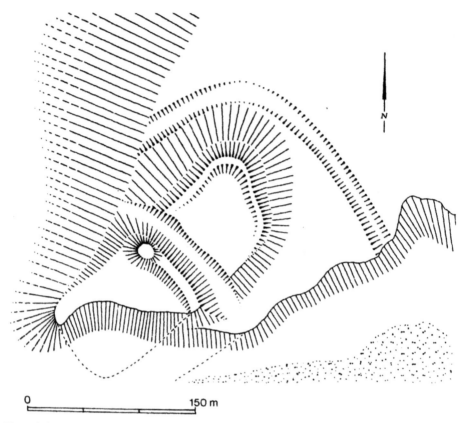

Plan of the earthworks of Hastings Castle, which sit on the cliff overlooking the modern town. Excavations here in the 1960s failed to find evidence of their Norman origins. (Higham *et al.* 1992)

as that shown on the Tapestry, this cannot be proved. In any case, the apparent use of a motte here contrasts strongly with the enclosure forms used elsewhere early in the Conquest, within earlier defences, at, for instance, Pevensey and Rochester. The Norman mound excavated at Hastings was dated by a single sherd of pottery and could have been built at any time after the Conquest. It is not even certain that it occupies the site chosen by William in 1066, since the seaward edge of the promontory on which it stands has suffered a long history of erosion. The castle shown on the Tapestry may have disappeared centuries ago. The excavated curtain wall was not built before the fourteenth century, though the debris of an earlier one was observed. Some of the expenditure in Henry II's reign was upon a keep, which has apparently disappeared into the sea. Some of this work (in 1181–83) was said to be upon the castle of 'New Hastings', perhaps indicating that the earlier site was already collapsing.

The scene has a number of other points of interest. The man giving instructions for the castle to be built (literally 'dug') might be Count Robert of Eu, to whom

A view of Hastings Castle c.1790, when the promontory on which it sat, known as 'The Gun', extended further south than it does today. The cliffs have been worn away by marine erosion and by deliberate clearance to accommodate the modern town.

Hastings was granted within a few years of the Battle of Hastings and with whom the twelfth-century Norman poet Wace associated its building. The men actually working on the castle, who might be Normans, or perhaps English prisoners pressed into labour, are supervised by a different overseer from the one who introduced the scene. Could this be Robert of Mortain, the duke's half-brother, who figures in the council of war shown immediately before the episode at Hastings? Or could it be Humphrey of Tilleul, whom Orderic Vitalis described as the first castellan of Hastings in the period before it was granted to Robert of Eu?

The castle is being constructed immediately next to a tall tower, shown on its right. It has been suggested that this represents a pre-Conquest church belonging to a Saxon community living within the Iron Age defences which excavation has revealed on the site. This community, wherever it was situated, is referred to in the Burghal Hidage list and in the *Anglo-Saxon Chronicle*. The present remains of the church are indeed very close to the remains of the motte. There is a parallel with Dover, which William subsequently fortified. Here also the prehistoric earthworks contained a Saxon church and settlement. There might also have been a similar arrangement at Pevensey.

Even if the detail of the superstructures is taken from contemporary illustrations, the depiction of earthen mottes suggests that the images may be based on first- or perhaps second-hand observation. As such they are significant visual representations of early motte-and-bailey castles, 'the first major monument of Anglo-Norman culture',[31] and despite reservations about their authenticity the Tapestry images remain an important testament to those monuments.

Chapter 5

The Oath

Perhaps the most significant episode in the whole of the Tapestry is the one that follows the depiction of Bayeux Castle. This scene, which occurs about halfway through, shows Earl Harold swearing an oath on holy reliquaries.

The Oath of Fealty

In the 790s, following a series of conspiracies and rebellions, feudal oaths of loyalty were instituted by Charlemagne, where all men were required to swear an oath of allegiance upon holy relics. The king's inner circle swore an even stronger oath of vassalage, committing them to obedience and military service. This was a binding covenant and breaking it was regarded as perjury. The precise details of what was sworn were not important; it was the oath itself that was sacrosanct.[1]

Catalonian nobles swore oaths to Count Raymond Berenguer I of Barcelona (1035–76) which invoked 'God and these holy things' and 'God and these his

Bayeux Tapestry. Earl Harold swearing an oath before his return to England. The close proximity of this scene to Bayeux Castle has been interpreted as an indication of where the episode took place, but some chroniclers suggest that it could have been elsewhere. Harold is standing on the cobbling, which is normally restricted to outside events, but here may represent the yet incomplete new cathedral at Bayeux.

saints'. In 1127 the citizens of Bruges swore fidelity to William Clito, Count of Flanders and King Louis VI of France on saints' relics and in return the count and king swore that they would observe the rights and privileges of the citizens of Bruges. In 1189 Richard I swore his coronation oath 'in front of the altar [in Westminster Abbey] in the presence of the holy gospels and the relics of many saints'.[2]

William of Poitiers claimed that Duke William hung the relics, on which the oath had been sworn, around his neck during the Battle of Hastings, thus calling up the power of the saints against the man he viewed as a perjurer:

> At his humble neck he [Duke William] hung the relics whose favour Harold had estranged from himself, having violated the oath which he had sanctified by swearing over them.[3]

Orderic Vitalis also records this episode and added that he attached the relics to his battle standard at Hastings.[4]

Among the gifts the Conqueror gave to Battle Abbey on its foundation in 1070 was a 'feretory in the shape of an altar, in which it was his custom to have mass said when on campaign'. It has been plausibly suggested that this was the portable reliquary shown on the Bayeux Tapesty.[5]

The sanctity of the oath was based on two things in medieval ceremonies: firstly, touching an object with the idea that the object would bring destruction if the oath was false, and secondly, invoking Divine witness to the event. God and the saints

Bayeux Tapestry. A close up view of Harold's oath, sworn on holy reliquaries.

would therefore not only be witnesses, but avengers as well.[6] Some authorities claim that the arrow in Harold's eye which killed him was a symbolic blinding – a direct consequence of his breaking a sacred oath. Recent analysis of the Tapestry has, however, suggested that this episode is suspect and the arrow penetrating Harold's eye may not have been part of the original Tapestry but was the result of later restoration of the needlework.[7]

On the Tapestry, Duke William, sitting on a throne decorated with an animal head on the arm and animal feet on the legs, is witnessing Earl Harold taking the oath with his hands on two sets of holy reliquaries. Reliquaries contained and displayed holy relics. It was believed that the body of a saint provided a spiritual link between life and death, between man and God: 'Because of the grace remaining in the martyr they were an inestimable treasure for the holy congregation of the faithful'.[8] As the relics themselves were considered 'more valuable than precious stones and more esteemed than gold', it was considered only appropriate that they be enshrined in vessels or reliquaries crafted in or covered by gold, silver, ivory, gems and enamel. Romanesque reliquaries were made in the form of caskets (Fr. *chasses*), thought originally to be based on the model of stone sarcophagi. Some reliquaries also resemble the shape of contemporary ecclesiastical buildings and can be thought of as miniature churches.[9] On the Tapestry, the abbey church of Mont-St-Michel could be interpreted as the form of a reliquary, nestled on a hilltop.

The Norman interpretation of the scene would have linked the oath with the earlier bestowing of arms, by which Harold had become William's vassal. The ritual oath completes the sequence which binds Harold to William by both custom and law. Others claim that it was no more than a proclamation of eternal friendship between two brothers in arms, while English commentators have argued that Harold probably swore the oath under duress and therefore it had no validity. Robert Wace (d.*c*.1174) went so far as to make the unlikely claim that Harold had no idea what was in the reliquary and therefore did not realize the full significance of what he was doing. Wace argues that William placed a chest full of relics under the altar cloth and when the relics were revealed after the oath had been sworn, Harold was deeply shocked. Wace implies that Harold was deceived into swearing the oath:

> To receive the oath, he caused a parliament to be called. It is commonly said that it was at Bayeux ... . He sent for all the holy bodies thither, and put so many of them together as to fill a whole chest, and then covered them with a pall; but Harold neither saw them, nor knew of their being there; for nought was shewn or told to him about it ... . When Harold placed his hand upon it, the hand trembled, and the flesh quivered; but he swore, and promised upon his oath, to take Ele to wife, and to deliver up England to the Duke ... after the death of Edward, if he should live, so help him God and the holy relics

there! Many cried, "God grant it" and when Harold had kissed the saints, and had risen upon his feet, the duke led him up to the chest, and made him stand near it; and took off the chest pall that had covered it, and shewed Harold upon what holy relics he had sworn; and he was sorely alarmed at the sight.[10]

The Tapestry shows the duke bearing his sword and pointing towards Harold and the relics. The only onlookers are ordinary soldiers and servants; such an event would normally be witnessed by clerical and secular lords. Perhaps, therefore, the Tapestry wanted to stress that this was a sacred bond between the two men and thus emphasize Harold's perfidy when he breaks it. William is accompanied by two men, one of whom holds a shield and a spear, while Harold stands alone between the two reliquaries. Both reliquaries are of the gabled, 'house shaped' variety and are adorned with five bays of Romanesque blind arcading. The arcades on both reliquaries are blind, but contemporary religious objects normally have figures set within each arch. On a portable square altar from Lower Saxony, commissioned in the 1030s by Countess Gertrude of Braunschweig, all four sides have arcading.

The front of the altar has a cloisonné enamel arcade with Christ in the centre and three Apostles on either side. The back panel mirrors the arrangement on the front, but here the arcades are worked in repoussé and the Apostles flank the Virgin Mary, her hands raised in a gesture of prayer and intercession. On one of the altar's sides are four sceptre-bearing angels under nielloed (compound black inlay) arcades flanking St Michael killing the dragon. On the remaining side the

Portable altar of the type found on the Tapestry made c.1045 for countess Gertrude of Braunschweig. (*Cleveland Museum of Art*)

emperor Constantine and his mother, Helena, are placed on either side of an enamelled cross, with the Burgundian king Sigismund and the Ottonian empress Adelheid following suit. It seems possible that the Bayeux Tapestry reliquaries were adorned with similar figures, possibly including Duke William.[11]

One of the reliquaries on the Tapestry, with cross-shaped finials, stands on a portable bier with two carrying poles from which textiles hang to the ground. The other has a central 'knob' on the ridge and is on a draped altar on three steps. Both the bier and the altar rest on a cobbled surface, suggesting that the oath took place in the open and that this altar was also movable.[12]

The reliquary to the right of Harold on the Tapestry is of a conventional rectilinear design, but the one to the left, between him and Duke William, has a curved lid in the shape of the hog's back roofs found on several buildings in the Tapestry. An early eleventh-century Danish reliquary, for which casts survive in the museums of Mainz and Copenhagen, is known to have had precisely this feature.[13]

According to two twelfth-century texts, the reliquary on which Harold swore his oath was known as the 'bull's eye' from the impressive round gemstone that adorned it. One of the sources, the *Hyde Chronicle*, probably written in Normandy in the 1130s, claimed that:

> Because Edward, the king of the English and a cousin on his mother's side to Duke William, did not have an heir, William granted the English kingdom to Harold on the condition that if Harold married William's daughter, he

A medieval hog's-back reliquary, similar in design to the left-hand reliquary on which Harold swears his oath.

would be forever faithful to William. When Harold agreed to this, he was immediately compelled to make strict oaths, because English loyalty was suspect, and a great number of sacred relics were ordered brought forth. Most important among the relics was the phylactery of St Pancras, which they call the 'ox eye' because its middle part contains a huge and beautiful gem. Harold took this phylactery knowing full well that so great a martyr could not be deluded by any rashness. And so, Harold came to the throne by an oath as strict as it was bold, and swore himself over the greatest token of the saints.[14]

St Pancras was a fourth-century martyr whose cult was centred on Rome, but although there were a number of churches dedicated to him in England, including one in Canterbury, he has no known association with Bayeux or indeed Normandy. It has been suggested that the 'huge and beautiful gem' of the shrine of St Pancras referred to in the chronicle could be the central jewel on top of one of the reliquaries in the Tapestry. It is possible that the Tapestry's designer may have confused St Pancras with St Pantaleon, whose relics are recorded in Bayeux Cathedral in the fifteenth century. More probably, any reference to St Pancras could have been linked to his role as patron saint of vows and treaties and in this case invoked against false

Medieval bull's-eye reliquary, possibly similar to that shown to the right of Harold on the Tapestry.

witness and perjury. Some historians have emphasized the symbolic importance of the 'bull's eye' shrine, linking it with sight and vision, which contrasted with Harold's own moral and supposed eventual physical blindness.

What exactly was sworn in the oath?

The Tapestry caption simply states, 'Where Harold took an oath to Duke William'. There has been much speculation about the contents of the oath as the Tapestry provides no further clue as to what was sworn. The most obvious explanation, as far as the general theme of the Tapestry is concerned, is that it was an oath of fealty or allegiance to William. The implication was that Harold would support William in his claim to the throne of England when Edward died. This would fit most closely with the Norman account of events which portrays Harold as a perjurer who broke his holy pledge and is subsequently justly defeated in battle. William's hagiographer, William of Poitiers, was in no doubt what was promised: Harold agreed to help William secure the English throne:

> He [Harold] pronounced clearly and of his own free will ... that he would be the agent of Duke William at the court of King Edward for as long as the king lived; that he would try with all his authority and power to ensure for him the possessions of the kingdom of England on Edward's death.[15]

William of Poitiers also claimed that Harold went even further with his promises and swore to hand over to William and his knights the castle (*castrum*) of Dover, fortified at Harold's own expense. Furthermore, he would build such other castles that William required in England and provide their garrisons with supplies. It seems probable that these promises at least were a product of the chronicler's imagination, but they underline the importance of Dover, both as a port and a fortification, in cross-Channel relations. Dover does not appear on the Tapestry, although it might have been in the final missing section as one of the locations which featured in William's march to London after the Battle of Hastings. William of Poitiers reported that the strongly fortified 'castle' at Dover occupied a rock adjoining the sea, but was no match for the Conqueror's troops. There was an earlier fortification here as well as a Roman lighthouse. William strengthened Dover' defences before he moved on to Canterbury in the autumn of 1066. Dover had been the site of Edward the Confessor's brother Alfred's fateful landing in 1036, after which he was captured and murdered. After Hastings Dover Castle was placed in the care of Bishop Odo and was unsuccessfully attacked by Eustace of Boulogne in 1067.

The twelfth-century *Hyde Chronicle* states that Harold would suffer as a result of his perjury – he could not 'provoke such a great martyr with impunity'. The 'Life of Edward the Confessor' describes Harold as 'too prone to oaths, more's the pity'. The chronicler of the abbey of Saint-Riquier in Ponthieu gratuitously credits Harold with another broken oath, by which he allegedly promised King Edward that he would promote the succession of Edgar Atheling, whose claim to the throne was in fact far stronger than either that of Harold or of William. It appears that Harold gained an unfortunate reputation for perjury even outside Normandy.

Where was Harold's oath sworn?

The importance of the oath scene within the Tapestry is one of few episodes of a specifically religious character within the embroidery. As a central and critical point in the story it is significant that it should be associated with the Church, and one building in particular, Bayeux Cathedral. This brings us to the question of precisely where the oath was sworn. The Tapestry seems to be fairly unequivocal, but there is no attempt to portray a specific building in which the event occurred. The critical scene follows on directly from the depiction of Bayeux Castle, but there is no suggestion that the castle is the end of a scene; there is no tree or tower marking a break in the story at this point. Instead the narrative flows smoothly and the contours of William's throne mirror those of the castle and are thus visually directly linked with the Bayeux fortification. If it is accepted that Bishop Odo was the sponsor of the embroidery, then Bayeux Cathedral, which Odo was in

The Romanesque crypt of Bayeux Cathedral built by Bishop Odo and consecrated in 1077.

the process of rebuilding, would have been the most appropriate place for this important event to take place.

Apart from the well-established links between St Augustine's Abbey and the creation of the Bayeux Tapestry, there were geographical contacts between Bayeux and Canterbury, which might explain the choice of Bayeux as the location for the oath.[16] Bayeux lies relatively close to the port of Caen from whence Caen stone was carried to England on a regular basis after the Conquest. Excavations at St Augustine's recovered large amounts of stone from Normandy and it has been estimated that 83 per cent of the stone from the abbey was Caen stone.[17] There is an interesting story told by the hagiographer Goscelin of Saint-Bertin during the stewardship of Abbot Scolland about the miracles of St Augustine. This tells of a convoy of fifteen ships carrying Caen building stone across the Channel which were caught in a storm, and all but the one bound for the new abbey of St Augustine sank. The importer was Bishop Odo's vassal, Vital of Canterbury, who actually appears on the Tapestry as the messenger who brings news of Harold's army before the Battle of Hastings.[18]

The depiction of the oath was at the heart of the Norman argument that Harold was a perjurer in the eyes of God. Locating it in the cathedral of Bayeux would have placed Bishop Odo at the centre of the story. There was probably no need for Odo to have been portrayed in this scene, as by implication it was taking place in Odo's own church.

The chroniclers disagree about where the oath was sworn. Robert Wace (c.1100–c.1174), who was also a canon of Bayeux Cathedral, writing almost a century after the events, placed the oath in Bayeux. The chronicler may have been echoing a local tradition, but he often seems to be accurate in his details despite the time lapse. He describes a solemn gathering of nobles and clerics around the relics, which Duke William had ordered 'to be assembled in one place'. Some years earlier William had apparently summoned relics from Rouen and elsewhere for the peace council that was held after the Battle of Val-ès-Dunes (1047), where he had defeated the rebel barons. The oath might have been associated with a similar peace council, summoned to determine the succession to the throne of England. A late twelfth-century account of the life of Thomas Becket locates the oath in the region of Bayeux, but at a hunting lodge called Bur-le-Roi.[19]

William the Conqueror's hagiographer, William of Poitiers, identifies Bonneville-sur-Touques as the place where the oath was taken. The castle here would have been on Harold's route from Bayeux to the coast of Lower Normandy, from where the earl would have sailed back to England. The coast between the Seine and the Orne estuaries, on which the Touques estuary lies, has been of particular historical significance. It was in the estuary of the River Dives, with its port of Dives-sur-Mer, that Duke William's invasion fleet was assembled before it moved northwards to another estuarine port at Saint-Valery-sur-Somme. It was also along this stretch of coast that Allied forces landed on D-Day in June 1944 at the start of the invasion of France. By the mid-twentieth century, none of the silted-up ports of the Bessin were large enough for the scale of the operation and therefore artificial ports, known as Mulberry harbours, had to be created.

There was a ducal castle at Bonneville, dating from 1059 to 1063, which could have been completed prior to Harold's expedition to Normandy. The castle which was close to the coast and the Touques and Seine estuaries was sited near to an area of Lower Normandy which had been traditionally troublesome for the dukes of Normandy. The castle would have overlooked the nearby port of Touques, which was conveniently close to William's fortified city of Caen and was regularly used by him later when king of England. Harold may well have sailed from here in 1064. The forest of Touques (later called the forest of Saint-Gatien) was adjacent to the duke's castle, probably extending as far as the River Risle to the east, and would have been an important hunting area for the dukes in the eleventh century. The abbey of Grestain, where William's mother was buried, lay less than 20km to the east of Touques. The castle is in the form of a fortified oval enclosure, surrounded by a deep ditch and positioned halfway up the north-east slope of the Touques valley. It is believed that the earliest fortifications here were of earth and timber and that most of the masonry now visible dates from the thirteenth century, although recent analysis of the structure showed that parts of the ramparts could have been eleventh century.[20]

Bonneville-sur-Touques was not associated with any holy shrines or relics, although the eleventh-century church of Saint-Pierre in the town of Touques

Aerial view of the ducal castle at Bonneville, one of the possible sites for Harold's oath. It appears that the original castle was in the form of a large ring-work fortification that subsequently had a stone rampart and bastions added.

The Romanesque church of St Pierre, Bonneville.

contains pre-Conquest features and might have been thought a suitable location for Harold taking the oath, immediately prior to his departure for England.

More probably, William of Poitiers's identification of Bonneville-sur-Touques as the location for the oath was prompted by his position as an archdeacon in the diocese of Lisieux, in which the castle was located. Bonneville was also the closest palace to the abbey of Préaux, where William had been a monk.

The other natural location for the oath was the ducal capital of Rouen. The Anglo-Norman chronicler Orderic Vitalis and the *Vita Haroldi* (*c*.1206) placed the oath near to Rouen, in the shade of an oak tree called the 'perjured tree'. There is no other evidence for Rouen having been the location, but the city did possess a large collection of relics, including those of St Ouen and St Catherine. If the Tapestry's chronology is correct then returning to England by way of Rouen would have involved the earl taking a long detour.

Bayeux Cathedral

The cathedral at Bayeux was second only to that at Rouen in importance in Normandy. Duke William had a specially designated chamber here, where it is known ducal charters were drafted.[21] The church sits in the south-east corner of the Gallo-Roman town of *Bajocassi*, earlier known as *Augustodurum*. In the third century the town was walled with a rectangular circuit of defences, which was destroyed in the eighteenth century, but the course of which can still be identified in the modern town plan. Under Bishop Odo (1049/50–87) its reputation was greatly enhanced as he increased its wealth and developed a vibrant cathedral chapter there. Bayeux Cathedral also became known as a centre of artistic achievement and learning under Odo's stewardship. Along with all the other ancient cathedrals in the archdiocese of Rouen, Bayeux was rebuilt during the eleventh century, but it was not consecrated until 1077; in which case it is likely that the oath was taken in the partly completed cathedral or the remnants of the Carolingian church, which had been attacked and badly damaged by Vikings. A replacement or restored church, about which we know nothing, was destroyed by fire in 1046 and work on a new cathedral was started by Odo's predecessor, Bishop Hugh (1001–1049).

Capital from Bishop Odo's eleventh-century cathedral at Bayeux recovered during building work in the nineteenth century.

Odo's new cathedral incorporated elements from an earlier group of Carolingian churches that had made up the pre-Viking cathedral. The choir was dedicated to Notre Dame and the nave to St Saviour; the latter also giving his name to the cathedral parish. A third church, dedicated to St Étienne, adjacent to the cathedral, survived until the seventeenth century.[22] It could well have been in one of these buildings that the oath was sworn. In 1856 a number of capitals which had been carved before the Conquest were found below later masonry at the crossing in the cathedral. Opinions on their artistic value vary, but they represent an important link with the earliest years of Odo's bishopric. The most unusual of the capitals is that which is believed to be one of the earliest representations of the Incredulity of Thomas.[23] The sculptors came from outside the duchy and were influenced by a variety of styles found from Provence to England. The presence of a cosmopolitan group of craftsmen confirms twelfth-century opinions of Bayeux 'which paint the city created by Odo as a centre of international trade and commerce'.[24] An early twelfth-century writer, Rodulf Tortaire, a monk of Fleury-sur-Loire, claimed that the cathedral was covered with statues. Although there is no other evidence for such decorative features, it is possible that the exterior did have a Romanesque frieze similar to that which survives at Lincoln Cathedral. The Lincoln frieze is, however, somewhat later, dating from Bishop Alexander's episcopacy (1123–48), although it is tempting to view the cartoon designs of this frieze in the context of the images on the Bayeux Tapestry. The surviving work from Odo's time shows that he operated on a grander and more lavish scale than his colleagues and 'indicates a monumentality, ambition, and stylistic range of reference of a quite remarkable kind'.[25]

Odo was responsible for other buildings associated with the cathedral, notably, the bishop's palace and the canons' houses. After its destruction by fire in 1046 the bishop's palace was moved to the north of the cathedral, where it has remained ever since. It seems to have been rebuilt at the same time as the cathedral as it was on the same alignment as the western towers. There are twelfth-century references to an *aula* (hall) and a *camera* (bishop's lodgings) in Odo's palace, and the palace appears to have had an L-shaped plan. Odo's palace was rebuilt after the 1105 fire.[26] Serlo described the 'precious chapter house' damaged by William the Conqueror's youngest son Henry I in 1105.[27] In the eleventh century the cathedral served the only parish within the walls of Bayeux, but there were a number of chapels, such as St Ouen in the castle and St Martin by the east gate, as well as the extramural suburban parish churches. Only the crypt and the bases of the two western towers survive from Odo's Romanesque cathedral, as much of the city and church were destroyed in 1105; the later cathedral seems to have followed the outline plan of Odo's building. It is also possible that the oath-taking took place in the abbey of St Vigor, outside the walled area of the city, which Bishop Odo was building at this time as his own intended mausoleum.

The Relics

In the eleventh century, holy relics represented the most precious possessions of a church. The veneration of relics rivalled the sacraments in the daily life of the medieval church and from the Second Ecumenical Council of Nicaca (AD787) it was obligatory for every altar to contain a relic. The body of a saint provided a spiritual link between life and death, and therefore a link between man and God. All relics bestowed honour and privileges upon their owner and became a lucrative attraction for those churches that possessed the most precious remains. Relics were kept in reliquaries, which were vessels crafted in or covered by gold, silver, ivory, gems and enamel.

There was a hierarchy in the importance of relics and those associated with the bodies and lives of Jesus Christ, the Virgin Mary and the Apostles were the most highly prized. Such relics gave those cathedrals, abbeys and churches holding them enormous status and created a powerful attraction for pilgrims. Of lesser importance were the relics of local saints, whose sanctity increased in proportion to the number of miracles associated with them. Although it was believed that saints might offer protection and perform miracles wherever they were venerated, they were at their most potent in the places where their bodies were preserved. It was believed that the gesture made by the taker of the oath demonstrated the presence of the 'sacred'. Sometimes, instead of laying hands on the reliquary, the oath-taker would stretch out their arms in supplication to Heaven.

As cathedrals and monasteries were being re-established in the wake of the Viking era in Western Europe, there was a scramble to reclaim dispersed relics or obtain new ones. This was particularly true of Normandy, where during the ninth century many relics had been dispersed, broken up or lost as a result of Viking attacks. Competition developed between the revived monasteries of the duchy to obtain sacred objects. There was also contention between the religious houses about the merits of different relics and as a result argument over the relative sanctity of neighbouring cathedrals. For example, Coutances Cathedral claimed that its dedication to the Virgin Mary was more sacred than that at Bayeux and, therefore, more worthy of veneration. There was even rivalry between institutions in the same city; for example, competition between the abbey of St Ouen and Rouen Cathedral over the importance of their relics sometimes resulted in violence.[28]

This friction was illustrated by the case of St Vigor (d.537), an early bishop of Bayeux, whose relics were the source of considerable contention. The remains of St Vigor were mainly held at St Riquier, where they had been taken in the tenth century after being displaced from Bayeux during the Viking period. According to the Chronicle of Hariulphe of St Riquier (d.1143), a cleric from Bayeux took St Vigor's relics from Bayeux around 987 and sold them to the abbey of St Riquier, where they remained and enjoyed considerable veneration. When Odo founded the monastery of St-Vigor-le-Grand just outside Bayeux in around 1066

St Vigor founded a monastery at Bayeux in the sixth century, which was restored by Bishop Odo as a Benedictine priory in the mid–eleventh century. It was intended to be the bishop's burial place, but he died in Palermo, where he was buried at the start of the First Crusade.

as an affirmation of the saint's ties to his episcopal city, he made strenuous, but unsuccessful, efforts to have the relics of St Vigor translated from St Riquier to Bayeux. The abbey of St Riquier was in Ponthieu, which, although subject to Duke William's overlordship, was not under any obligation to Bayeux. The monks of St Riquier argued that Bayeux should have taken better care of its relics in the first place and refused to return them.

The relics belonging to St Exuperius (*c*.390–405), the first bishop of Bayeux, had been moved to Corbeil, on the Seine to the south of Paris, for safety. Bishop Odo was again involved in an unsuccessful and humiliating episode attempting to repatriate the remains of Exuperius to Bayeux. As part of his efforts to establish a relic cult at Bayeux, Odo attempted to bribe the sacristan of Corbeil to give him the bones of St Exuperius which, apart from the head and a tooth, had been moved from Bayeux. This shabby tale was related by Guibert of Nogent in his *Treatise on Relics* of 1106:

> Odo, Bishop of Bayeux, eagerly desired the body of St Exuperius ... . He paid, therefore, the sum of one hundred pounds to the sacristan of the church which possessed these relics that he might take them for himself. But the sacristan cunningly dug up the bones of a peasant named Exuperius and brought them to the Bishop.

The custodian swore on oath that these were the authentic bones of the saint, but Guibert records how the townspeople of Bayeux were incensed by what they saw as a betrayal of their patron saint: 'See now what disgrace this Bishop's bargain brought upon religion when the bones of this profane peasant Exuperius were thrust upon God's holy altar, which perchance will never more be purged of them'.[29]

Probably after this event Odo commissioned a new shrine in his cathedral for two obscure British saints, Rasyphus and Ravennus, whose cult was the most popular at Bayeux in the mid-eleventh century. The two saints were brothers who fled from the Anglo-Saxon invasions of England in the fifth century. They travelled to Macé in France where they were eventually martyred. At some stage they were moved from Macé to Saint-Vaast-sur-Seulles (Calvados), south of Bayeux. In the early eleventh century the location of the bodies was revealed to Bishop Hugh of Bayeux, who, after the saints insisted on a change of scenery, oversaw their translation and enshrinement at Bayeux.

Subsequently, the cult of the two saints flourished. Although the story that supplied their pedigree was a Norman fabrication, as fifth-century martyrs, Rasyphus and Ravennus provided a high-status devotional focus. Their feast day was celebrated in the cathedral and their altar was second only to the high altar, dedicated to the Virgin Mary. Bishop Odo's centrepiece for the shrine was a new reliquary, which is described in an inventory of 1476 as a large architectural shrine, richly decorated with gilding and enamel work.

> The back side [of the shrine] is of gilded silver or worked in beaten metal; and all the rest of it, that is to say the front side, the two ends, and the top is made of fine gold, with raised golden images, and decorated with large and expensive enamels and precious stones of various kinds.[30]

The reliquary was installed on an especially dedicated altar in the apse of Bayeux Cathedral just behind the primary altar and was described by a sixteenth-century antiquarian as 'a miniature version of Bayeux Cathedral that was taller than a ten-year-old girl'.[31]

Although the cult of the brothers did not spread outside Bayeux, at the time Harold swore his oath their perceived sanctity would have been at its height and their fine new reliquary would have provided an appropriately holy shrine for the purpose. It is also clear from what we know of Odo in other contexts that he would not have hesitated to use the opportunity of the Tapestry to advertise the Bayeux cult to an audience outside his own diocese.[32]

Odo was also involved with relics at Canterbury where he was a friend and benefactor of St Augustine's Abbey. When Abbot Scolland was rebuilding the abbey in the 1070s, the bishop advised him on moving St Hadrian's sarcophagus from the old church without disturbing the bones. Odo also participated in the process of translating the relics of St Augustine and other saints into the abbey's new church. The monk Goscelin, writing in the 1090s, described how Odo had given the community excellent and successful advice about how they should move the relics. The inclusion of Odo in St Augustine's Martyrology, after he died in 1097, confirms that he was still remembered in the monks' prayers, despite having been exiled by William II.[33]

The Return Journey

Immediately after the oath scene Harold returns to England. Indeed, one of the attendants watching the earl's oath already has one foot in the wavy lines which are employed to depict the sea throughout the Tapestry. Harold's boat is of familiar design with round shields again projecting above the gunwale, with the earl once more at the helm. The whole episode is contracted into a single scene and shows the boat being sighted by a lookout guard in England at the same time as it is

Bayeux Tapestry. Harold returns to England and lands at what appears to be a grander port than Bosham, it is possibly meant to depict Portchester or Southampton.

leaving Normandy, while the sail is being lowered for landing. The text simply reports that, 'Here Duke Harold returned to the English land'.

The lookout appears to be standing on an ornate balcony of a building on piers that face out towards Harold's incoming ship. There is an animal head adorning the end of the balcony, projecting out to sea, as if in harmony with the attendant guard. This feature suggests that part of the structure, at least, was built of timber. The building appears to represent a substantial town house, looking on to a street by means of an archway. Three faces peer out to sea from three first-storey windows. Another face looks out from the only window on a second floor, above which there is a hog's-back roof with decorated shingle tiles. It has been suggested that this building is similar to one described in the Oseney Abbey Cartulary as 'a shop with a sun-roof above and a cellar below'.[34] However, there is no evidence of a cellar on the Tapestry. In fact, it looks more like a port building with a pier projecting out to sea at which boats could moor. The whole scene implies a more structured harbour than that at Bosham. The major ports along the south and south-east coasts of England where ships from Normandy could have expected to land at this time were Dover, Sandwich and Southampton. Another possibility is Portchester, 5km to the north-west of Portsmouth, which became a favourite point of departure for royalty during the later Middle Ages.

Portchester, like Pevensey, was a fort of the Saxon Shore first built by the Romans in the third century and was called *Portus Adurni* in the *Notitia Dignitatum*, a late

The Roman fort of the Saxon Shore at Portchester from the air. The fort was later used as a favoured departure place for medieval monarchs.

Roman document which details imperial diplomatic missions. The Saxon Shore forts were a series of substantial stone fortresses along the south-east and east coasts of England. They are usually sited at the entrance to large estuaries, which served as harbours for naval units. Each fort had massive stone defences strengthened by projecting bastions and was entered through narrow gateways. During the late Saxon period it became a *burh*, one of the sites fortified by Alfred the Great against the Vikings. Recent geophysical work at Portchester has identified a jetty used for offloading vessels.[35] Portchester lies only a few kilometres to the west of Bosham, where Harold's expedition had begun.

The final stage of the events of 1064 on the Tapestry sees Harold reporting back to King Edward. There is no indication of where this scene took place, apart from that it was in one of Edward's palaces, presumably either Westminster or Winchester. However, this palace is far simpler in design than the one from which Harold had departed. It seems to be supported only by wooden columns and capitals and therefore could have been one of the king's lesser palaces. On the top of the hog's-back roof there are two pepper-pot towers and between these there is a curious structure which looks like a small two-storey building in its own right. With the towers it projects into and fills the upper border. The structure has an awkwardly shingled roof with a feathery-looking roof finial.

Bayeux Tapestry. Harold reports back to King Edward.

Edward is shown seated, not on a throne as before, but on a long bench with a cushioned top; he is accompanied by an attendant holding a housecarl's battleaxe. He is wearing the same robes and insignia as in the opening scene of the Tapestry. The king seems to have aged markedly during the earl's absence by the appearance of his grey beard and seems to be reprimanding Harold. The earl is accompanied by an attendant also holding a housecarl's battleaxe, and appears to be bowing his head, perhaps in shame. The text is of no help as it simply states 'and came to King Edward'. This is another enigmatic scene that may be referring to circumstances for which we have no other information. Orderic Vitalis claimed that Harold told the king that William had refused to accept the crown and given it up to the earl. Harold was also supposed to marry William's daughter and thus become the duke's son-in-law. Orderic says that Edward was surprised by the decision, but accepted this story and gave his approval to Harold the 'clever tyrant'. One possible explanation for Harold's bowed figure could be that it was a simple mistake by the embroiderer, who had to keep the scene within the central narrative but had overestimated the space available and was obliged to portray Harold in a bent position. Another peculiarity of this scene is that Harold and his attendant are standing between a tower and the palace, apparently outside the building. This contrasts with the opening scene of the Tapestry when Harold and his men are shown inside the palace with the king. The men are standing on the cobbled surface design that normally depicts exterior scenes, while Edward is clearly seated within the palace. This distinction between the two men may have been intended to demonstrate Harold's new outsider status and perhaps indicate Edward's displeasure that Harold's mission had not gone as the king would have wished.

Chapter 6

Westminster

The next few scenes in the Tapestry are centred on Westminster. In the eleventh century, Westminster was quite separate from London, which in the late Saxon era was largely contained within the area of the old Roman walled town. There were two kilometres or so of open ground between the city and Westminster. Today, Westminster is dominated by the Houses of Parliament and Westminster Abbey, but late Saxon Westminster occupied Thorney Island, which was an eyot in the Thames. This island of sand and gravel was formed by rivulets of the River Tyburn, which flowed down from where Regent's Park now lies. The Tyburn joined the Thames near the lowest point where it could be forded from the north bank at low tide. Thorney Island still existed in the Middle Ages and vestiges of it survived until the eighteenth century.

Westminster Abbey

The Tapestry first features a splendid depiction of Westminster Abbey church, into which the body of King Edward is being carried from right to left, a reversal

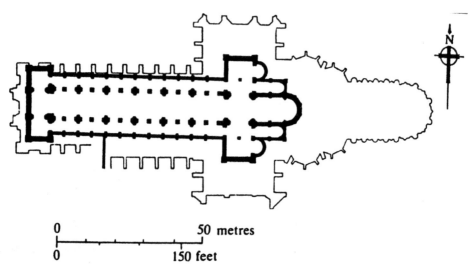

Plan of Edward the Confessor's Westminster abbey church (bold) compared to the modern church. This reconstruction of the eastern end of the eleventh century church has recently been questioned. (*Woodman 2015*)

of the normal consecutive left to right narrative employed in most of the rest of the Tapestry.

On the Tapestry, Edward's death scene follows after his burial, apparently out of sequence, but, if this group of scenes was deliberately meant to be read right to left, it makes sense. Immediately afterwards, the newly crowned King Harold is seen sitting in majesty on a throne in Westminster Palace. The new king's splendour is soon cruelly punctured by a sighting of Halley's Comet, a portent of disaster ahead.

The church is seen from the north side, but as in some other buildings on the Tapestry, combines interior and exterior features in a single view. To the right is the nave, consisting of five bays, with a row of windows above. The nave has a roof covered with large rectangular tiles, probably lead, as Edward's *Vita* describes 'a wooden roof which is carefully covered in lead'. There is a carved floral finial at the west end. In the centre stands the crossing, depicted as a large arch which supports a grand lantern tower, which itself is flanked by bell towers. The Vita talks of 'a tower reaching up with spiralling stairs in artistic profusion'. To the east of the tower, a staircase is shown in various colours leading up to the choir. To the left, the apse is relatively plain apart from a floral finial at the east end of its roof.

Although the abbey church at Westminster was not completed until 1090, its consecration coincided with the dramatic events at the end of 1065 and the

Bayeux Tapestry. Westminster Abbey.

beginning of 1066. The church was the first Romanesque building to be completed in England. William of Malmesbury observes that 'the king built it in that style which he was the first in England to use but which now [*c*.1125] all seek to emulate at vast expense'.[1] It would almost certainly have been the largest church in the country at that time. Indeed, with an internal length of 98.2m (322ft), it was markedly bigger than the great churches being then built in Normandy and larger even than that at Chartres in France. King Edward's Westminster was closer in scale to the great imperial churches of the Rhineland, such as Mainz (started *c*.975) and Speyer (started 1030). His ambitions for his church and mausoleum had clearly been influenced by his long years in exile in France. During his time in the ducal household in France between 1016 and 1041, Edward would have witnessed the early phases of the monastic revival and the introduction of Romanesque architecture into Normandy. He would also have been influenced by his contact with Continental clerics from further afield. At Westminster, Edward wanted to promote his royal image both in life and in death. Not only did he build the grandest church in the kingdom, he created a great political, economic and intellectual centre, with a royal palace and a great hall sited within the same compound.

The neo-classical style of architecture that developed into Romanesque had spread from Burgundy into Normandy under the influence of clerics such

Westminster Reconstruction showing the abbey and palace at Westminster at the end of the eleventh century. The palace had been rebuilt by William II, close to the site of Edward's building. (*Terry Ball*)

The Sacramentary or Missal of Robert of Jumièges given by him as a memorial of himself to the monastery of Jumieges when he was Bishop of London. The cavalry riders at the bottom of the picture are riding towards a fortified town. (*Rouen City Library*)

The remains of Jumièges Abbey, consecrated in 1067 in the presence of William the Conqueror.

as William of Volpiano, abbot of Fécamp between 1001 and 1031. Although Westminster was clearly Edward's church, the inspiration for the design may have come from Robert II, Abbot of Jumièges, who had travelled to England from Normandy with Edward in 1042.

Robert became Bishop of London (1044–51) and later Archbishop of Canterbury (1051–52). Robert, who would have been involved in the planning of the new abbey church at Jumièges (1040–67) in the Seine valley, may have transferred some of his ideas on Romanesque design to Westminster. In 1052 he fled from England on the return of Godwin, Earl of Wessex from exile. Godwin was largely responsible for declaring Robert an outlaw and deposing him as prelate in the same year.

Excavations on the west side of the cloisters, in what would have been the cellarer's range at Westminster, in 2010–12 revealed the earliest structure yet found on the abbey site. Evidence of occupation from the mid Saxon period onwards was uncovered together with the chalk rubble foundations of a late tenth-century rectangular building.[2] Earlier investigation in the church uncovered the lower part of the north wall of the choir and part of the main apse. The choir consisted of two bays with solid side walls ending in a semicircular east end. The surviving remains of early monastic buildings indicate that the crossing and the transepts occupied the same position as those features in the later building. Earlier archaeological work in 1930 laid bare the western part of the south arcade of the nave and the

Westminster Abbey Romanesque undercroft. One of the few surving parts of the abbey dating from Edward the Confessor's construction.

south-west tower. The nave would seem to have consisted of six double bays with alternate cruciform and square piers.[3]

Hardly any surviving elements of Edward's church can be seen today, apart from the round arches and massive supporting columns of the undercroft and the Pyx Chamber in the cloisters. The undercroft originally provided accommodation for the monks and it would therefore appear that work was progressing on the monastic precinct as well as the church before the Conquest. Recent analysis of the undercroft has confirmed that the earliest structure is no later than the 1060s and that the walls and vault preserve the earliest suite of masons' marks in England. The pavement of the chamber has been patched with reused large brown glazed tiles with hand-incised designs. Similar tiles, which were used as packing material and gap fillers in the earliest masonry in the undercroft, have been dated to the 1060s or earlier and thus represent some of the earliest decorated floor tiles found in England. Dendrochronological analysis of a battered oak door hanging in the chapter-house vestibule dated it to the 1050s, confirming a long-held belief that it was also a survival from the Confessor's Abbey.[4]

Richard Gem has provided the following description of Westminster Abbey from King Edward the Confessor's *Vita*.

And so, at the king's command the work, notably begun, is being prepared successfully; and neither the outlay nor what is to be expended are weighed, so long as it proves worthy and acceptable to God and blessed Peter. The house of the principal altar, raised up with very high arches (or vaults), is surrounded with squared work and even jointing; moreover, the periphery of the building itself is enclosed on either side by a double arch of stones, strongly consolidated with a joining together of work from different directions. Further on is the crossing of the temple; which might surround the central quire of those singing to God, and with its twin abutment from different directions might support the lofty apex of the central tower; it rises simply, at first with a low and strong vault (or arch); grows, multiple in art, with many ascending spiral stairs; then indeed, reaches with a plain wall right up to the wooden roof, carefully roofed with lead: indeed, disposed below and above, lead out chapels, fit to be consecrated by means of their altars to the memories of the apostles, martyrs, confessors and virgins. Moreover, this multiplicity of so vast a work is set out so great a space from the East (end) of the old temple that, of course, in the meantime the brethren staying therein might not cease from the service of Christ; and furthermore so that some part of the nave to be placed between might advance.

Edward's church at Westminster was built of Reigate dressed stone. Its nave had six double bays, two bays longer than that at Jumièges; the Tapestry shows only five bays. The ground arcade in the nave was defined by great compound piers, each divided by a pair of round arches resting on a plain cylindrical column. This

A reconstruction of the Romanesque church of St Benign, Dijon.

pattern of alternating massive and simple piers could be seen at Bishop Odo's church at St Vigor in Bayeux and may have its origins at St Bénigne in Dijon.

The eastern section beyond the crossing was made up of two bays. There may also have been a western porch which connected the old church to the new. According to a later poem, there were two western towers, but these may not have been completed at the time the Tapestry was made; a concept supported by the fact that some of the masonry surviving within the towers dates from the later eleventh century.[5]

The conventional interpretation of Edward's design has been challenged by Woodman, who suggests that the comparisons should be made not so much with Jumièges, but with Rouen Cathedral which was consecrated in 1065. This building was started by the immensely influential Robert II, Archbishop of Rouen and Count of Evreux (*c*.989–1037). Robert was Edward the Confessor's uncle as well as William the Conqueror's great-uncle and protector during his early years as duke of Normandy. Woodman argues that the east end of Edward's Westminster Abbey was more complex than traditionally thought, and consisted of an apse, ambulatory and radiating chapels. With these additions to the generally accepted plan, 'Westminster Abbey would truly have been the fountainhead of Anglo-Norman architecture in the post-Conquest period. It could have provided the model for Battle Abbey, St Augustine's Canterbury, St Paul's in London and Norwich Cathedral.'[6]

Westminster Abbey church was due to be consecrated on Christmas Day 1065, but the ceremony was postponed because King Edward fell ill and it was delayed until 28 December, by which time it had become obvious that Edward was not going to be in a fit condition to attend. The *Vita* explains how the w*itan* was already assembled at Westminster for the double celebration of Christmas and the consecration. Thus, 'When that celebrated day, which the blessed passion of the Holy Innocents adorns, had come, the excellent prince ordered them to hasten on with the dedication of the church and not to put it off again'.[7]

The *Anglo-Saxon Chronicle* reported that 'the minster which Edward had himself built, to the honour of God and St Peter, and all God's saints' was attended by clerics and noblemen 'from the whole of Britain'. The Tapestry does not specifically depict the consecration ceremony, which was conducted by Archbishop Stigand; however, the church is symbolically 'consecrated' by a builder performing the traditional 'topping-out' ceremony by placing a weathercock on the roof at the eastern end of the building. This was a convention that dated from at least the tenth century, confirmed by a letter from Bishop Wulfstan of London, written about 993, which refers to a golden cock on top of Winchester Cathedral. Also the hand of God is shown above the nave either blessing the church or, perhaps anticipating the next scene, welcoming the 'saintly' Edward to Heaven.[8]

The Death of King Edward the Confessor

Edward's death scene is set in the Palace of Westminster, next to the abbey church, where King Edward was staying when he fell ill. The general consensus of opinion is that he suffered a stroke. The depiction of the palace is reminiscent of the very first scene of the Tapestry. On the left is a turret, apparently foreshortened, consisting of one and a half storeys; possibly it represents a covered stairwell leading to the first floor, where the king is bedridden. On the right there is a more regular double tower, which also appears to incorporate a covered stairway. There are steps around the base of both structures.

The king appears to be lying in a four-poster bed, surrounded by draperies which frame the king but are loosely tied around the bedposts. One of the bedposts has a carved dragon head on top. Edward, who is identified by his crown, is obviously very ill. The king's steward of the Palace of Westminster, Robert fitz Wimarc, is propping Edward's head up on a cushion. Wimarc, also known as the Staller, was a Norman who had arrived in England with Edward on his return from exile and reputedly had built a castle at Clavering (Essex) by 1052. He later advised Duke William to return to France in the face of what he argued were the impossible odds of defeating Harold. Despite this he remained in favour with William and became sheriff of Essex after the Conquest.[9]

At Edward's bedside are three other clearly identifiable figures: Archbishop Stigand is standing next to the king and is holding up his hands either in an expression of despair or in a blessing for the dying monarch; Earl Harold is kneeling and touching fingers with Edward; and Queen Edith, Edward's wife and

Bayeux Tapestry. Edward the Confessor's funeral cortège reaches Westminster.

Pilgrims being cured at the shrine of Edward the Confessor c.1250, from 'Life of St Edward the Confessor' by Mathew Paris. (*Cambridge University Library*)

Harold's sister, is weeping into her veil. The accompanying text states, 'Here King Edward speaks with his followers on his bed, and here he died.' The *Vita* confirms that these three were indeed there, along with Robert fitz Wimarc.

There is no overall agreement how the death scene should be interpreted, although many historians believe that it shows Edward passing on the crown to Harold before he died. This view is supported by the Anglo-Saxon Chronicle, which states that Edward bequeathed the crown to Harold. According to the *Vita*,

Bayeux Tapestry. A detailed view of Edward's death-bed scene, which appears on the tapestry after the funeral.

before he died Edward took counsel with his immediate advisers and bequeathed the throne to Harold, with the stipulation that he should protect Queen Edith and her lands, saying, 'I commend this woman and the entire kingdom to your protection.' Edward also provided for those Frenchmen who had remained with him after Earl Godwin had regained dominance in 1052. He instructed Harold to accept an oath of loyalty from those who wanted to stay in England and retain them in his service. Those who wished to return to France should be allowed to do so, taking their possessions, under safe conduct.[10]

Edward's options in his choice of successor were strictly limited. According to Saxon tradition, the new king should be a blood relative, however remote. Additionally, the candidate should have sufficient support within the *witan*, that is, the leading *eoldermen* in the kingdom. There was only one serious legitimate English blood contender, the fourteen-year-old Prince Edgar, son of Edward the Exile and grandson of King Edmund II Ironside. Despite his credentials as Edward the Confessor's grand-nephew, he had only recently returned from exile in Hungary and would not have been known to the *witan*; he was also deemed too young to take on the challenging role of king in the then prevailing political circumstances. Edgar the Atheling, as he was conventionally known, was made Earl of Oxford by Harold after his coronation, a title he lost two years later when he rebelled against the Conqueror. During the interregnum between Harold's death and William's coronation, Edgar was regarded as the *de facto* king.

By offering the crown to someone outside the royal lineage, Edward opened the way for Duke William's continued involvement in the succession. The Norman chroniclers claim that Edward was confirming William's claim to the throne and, even if the kingdom was bequeathed to Harold, it was only to keep it safe while awaiting the arrival of the duke.

Edward died during the night of 4–5 January 1066 and the lower half of the same scene shows Edward's corpse being tended to in the presence of a priest, possibly Archbishop Stigand. The juxtaposition of the image of the dead king below his living image above makes it look as if he is now on the ground floor or undercroft, but this is probably a shorthand method of putting the two scenes in the bedroom together. The two images share the upright posts, but in the lower section they are clearly structural posts rather than bedposts. Edward no longer wears his crown but appears to have a skullcap on his head, which rests on a plain white pillow, giving the appearance of a halo. The king's body is wrapped in a dark winding sheet, which may have been made from leather, as was contemporary practice for high-ranking individuals.[11] For example, after William the Conqueror died at Rouen in 1087, he was wrapped in ox hide for his journey to Caen for burial.

The death of a king was a significant religious and cultural event and the Tapestry records the ceremony with due care for detail. The importance of the death scene is enhanced as it is the only visual representation of a royal burial from the period. No other surviving contemporary manuscript depicts a funeral cortège in this way and it seems probable that the Tapestry's designer took these images from real life.[12]

The funeral cortège is shown leaving for the abbey church on the left-hand side of the death scene. Edward's exposed body, wrapped in its shroud, is carried on an ornate funeral bier, which is covered in precious cloths and has a cross at either end. The king is accompanied by the tonsured religious community of Westminster Abbey, some of whom are singing. Two of the monks appear to be holding books, presumably sacred texts. One has his hand facing inwards, pressed against his chest in a gesture of sorrow. These might be members of the royal chapel, several of whom were Normans who had accompanied Edward to England in 1041. They also probably represent the *witan* and the housecarls. The text states, 'Here the corpse of King Edward is borne to the church of the Apostle Saint Peter.' Two of the boys carry bells, one in each hand, giving notice of the approach of the corpse, to ring out the elevated status of the man who is to be buried and to frighten off the Devil. The ringing of bells was a customary feature of burials both in England and in Normandy. Three of the pall-bearers have staves, which differ from the crosier-like staff carried by the first monk. The staves would have been used to strike the ground with the approach of the royal corpse.

The elaborately decorated bier on which Edward is being carried is of particular significance. It has been suggested that the crosses on the bier could have indicated the Confessor's saintly status. Alternatively, they may have formed part of a portable

Bayeux Tapestry. The death of King Edward portrayed as two episodes, one on top of the other. In the upper scene Edward, on his deathbed is surrounded by his wife Edith, Archbishop Stigand, Robert Wimarc and Earl Harold, to whom he appears to be passing the throne.

reliquary or feretory. Subsequent kings, including William the Conqueror, Henry I and Henry III, seem to have been carried to their tombs in a similar manner. The *Vita Eadwardi* explains that Edward's body was to be interred 'with the singing of masses and the relief of the poor' and accompanied by much wailing from the mourners. During the day and night preceding the interment, Edward's body had rested at Westminster, where 'prayers and sighs and psalms were offered up' throughout the vigil. Subsequently, in the thirty days following the event, masses were celebrated and psalms chanted and more gifts were provided for the poor and 'for the redemption of Edward's soul'.

When Edward's sepulchre was opened in 1685, remains of his silk clothing were found together with a richly enamelled gold crucifix hanging on a gold chain and a diadem of gold. The tomb had earlier been opened in 1102 when it was recorded that the grave contained a gold crown, a sceptre, a gold ring and ceremonial sandals.[13] Although the Tapestry does not show these items, they are consistent with the solemn and sophisticated character of the funeral process depicted. Edward was the first of many monarchs to be buried at Westminster, unlike his predecessors, who were mostly buried at Winchester. Edward's body was interred in a stone sarcophagus sunk into the pavement immediately before the high altar. Edward was canonized in 1161 and the body was 'translated' (moved) to a new tomb. He was moved again in 1269, when a magnificent new shrine was consecrated in Henry III's rebuilt church, and a much reduced version of this still occupies St Edward's Chapel to the east of the Sanctuary.

King Harold

The Bayeux Tapestry portrays what is normally interpreted as Harold's coronation and implies that it was undertaken with the consent of the secular and ecclesiastic communities. To the right of Edward's death scene, Harold is offered the crown by two unidentified men, but whose rank is indicated by the housecarl's battleaxe one of them carries. These men represent the *witan*, which had the ultimate say in the succession, but the event appears to have been outdoors with no cleric present. The accompanying caption simply says, 'Here they gave the king's crown to Harold.' This version of events is supported by the account of John of Worcester (d.*c*.1140): 'After the burial the underking Harold, Earl Godwine's son, whom the king before his death had appointed successor to the kingdom, was elected to the royal dignity by the magnates of the whole realm and on the same day was honourably consecrated king by Ealdred, Archbishop of York.'[14] The Norman chroniclers William of Jumièges and William of Poitiers both contest this version of events, claiming that Harold seized the throne unlawfully and, furthermore, that he was crowned by the discredited Archbishop of Canterbury, Stigand. On the Tapestry, it is implied that Stigand alone crowned Harold. The archbishop had been excommunicated by several popes and was guilty of simony and pluralism as he held the see of Winchester at the same time as Canterbury. The Norman view was that Stigand was not the authentic archbishop and therefore any blessing he might bestow on Harold on behalf of the Church was not legitimate.

In the following scene Harold appears in great splendour as the new king. The crown Harold is offered is different from the one he is seen wearing later and the one worn by Edward. The text, ambiguous as ever, says, 'Here they gave the king's crown to Harold.' The convention followed by the *witan* was that it selected the best qualified man from the House of Wessex. In normal circumstances this would have been the deceased king's eldest son, but Edward's closest male kin was the young Edgar Atheling. The *witan* seems to have had little choice as Harold was clearly the most powerful man in the kingdom and, although he was not of royal blood, his sister had been Edward's queen.

The next scene sees Harold in the coronation ceremony, where he shows himself to his subjects. It takes place in a palace, presumably Westminster, which is depicted with the usual side stair turrets, a hog's-back roof and three pepper-pot dormers. Harold is seated on a high throne, wearing a crown which has had the fleur de lys, missing from an earlier scene, restored, and is holding the sceptre and orb of state. To the left, two laymen offer the new king a sword, the symbol

Bayeux Tapestry. Harold's coronation with Archbishop Stigand clearly identified as being responsible for crowning the new king. The scene appears to be located in a palace rather than the abbey.

Bayeux Tapestry. Archbishop Stigand of Canterbury (1052–1070).

of temporal power, while to the right stands Stigand. The archbishop is wearing a chasuble with plain banding and a long pallium, which had been given to him by the antipope Honorius II (d.1072), decorated with a dot and cruciform motif; in his left hand he is holding a plain stole with decorative bands at either end. Although it is not explicitly stated what ceremony he is performing, his open arms suggest that he is welcoming Harold on behalf of the Church.

By the mid eleventh century, the coronation ceremony had become of supreme importance in transforming a man into a king. The royal regalia would have included gloves, sandals, a tunic and a stole. The new monarch would have carried a sceptre, rod and orb. In return for the anointment of the king, the Church expected peace and protection.

Although Edward had wanted to be buried at Westminster, he may not have intended the building to have become England's coronation church. Like many of his predecessors he had been crowned at Winchester Cathedral and *force majeure* dictated that Harold should be crowned as quickly as possible after Edward's death. He would have needed to emphasize continuity with his predecessor's reign – Westminster Abbey was at hand and therefore immediately used to crown the new king. Every monarch since 1066 has been crowned at Westminster apart from Edward IV and Edward VIII who did not have coronations.

Outside the palace, to the right, five laymen view the proceedings, representing the element of popular acclamation which was a traditional feature of contemporary succession and coronation rituals. The text reads, 'Here sits Harold, King of the English. Archbishop Stigand.' As with many scenes in the Tapestry, this one can be read in several ways: on the one hand, it represents the people and the Church accepting Harold; while on the other, it links Harold's kingship to Stigand, the archbishop considered a usurper by the Normans.

Stigand's situation after the Conquest was problematic. Undoubtedly, the archbishop was closely associated with the Godwinsons and regarded as a pluralist, representative of the worst excesses of the Saxon Church in the eyes of the Normans. On the other hand, he represented the continuity that William wanted immediately after 1066. Stigand remained archbishop until 1070 and was eventually removed from office not by the king, but by papal legates. It has even been suggested that Stigand played a role in the creation of the Bayeux Tapestry.[15] William may have been unwilling to unseat an archbishop, even one widely seen as a usurper. More probably, the king hesitated because in the first instance he wished to form an alliance with the English Church and aristocracy. This policy altered significantly after the uprisings of the late 1060s, after which William replaced almost every English bishop and abbot with his own choice of Continental clerics.

The Comet

The next scene shows a group of laymen outside the palace drawing attention to a heavenly body that appears in the upper border. Following contemporary literary

Bayeux Tapestry. Halley's Comet sighted immediately after Harold's coronation. The new king is visibly deflated by the news.

tradition this object is depicted as a moving star with a fantail. The men may have been part of the same group who, immediately before, had been giving the acclamation, but this time there are six of them. The body language of the two groups of men is linked together as attention is drawn from Harold towards the comet. The text explains that, 'They wonder at the star.' The designer is using artistic licence; although Halley's Comet did appear in 1066, it was visible between 14 April and 8 June and, therefore, not close to Harold's coronation. In the late

Bayeux Tapestry. Ghost ships in the border beneath the scene where Harold is told of the appearance of Halley's Comet.

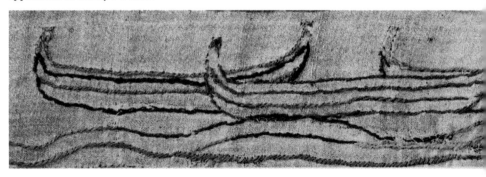

Saxon period, the appearance of a comet was interpreted as a portent of change, normally a catastrophe; famine, plague or war could be expected to follow. For instance, a record of the sighting of a comet by the *Anglo-Saxon Chronicle* for 975 was followed by a severe famine. The appearance of Halley's Comet in 1066 was connected to other disasters, not just Harold's defeat at Hastings but, for example, Icelandic chronicles associate its appearance with Harald Hardrada's defeat at Stamford Bridge. The *Anglo-Saxon Chronicle* reported the appearance of the comet with the conclusion that it would bring ill fortune for some. The *Chronicle* declared that nothing like it had been seen in the heavens before and linked it to a hostile landing, by Harold's half-brother Tostig, on the Isle of Wight in May 1066. There was a common feeling that the comet was linked to Harold's downfall and this was expressed in a saying that was soon in popular circulation, 'In 1066 the English felt the lash of the comet's tail.'

Baudri's poem, written sometime after 1080, also mentions the appearance of the comet, but is imprecise about the timing and is enigmatic about its meaning:

Behold the sky flashes, now flashes the reddening comet;
with spreading rays it glitters towards the people ...
Mothers suckling their darling babes
strike both breast and mouth and dread new portents.[16]

The written source which comes closest in its description to the Tapestry image is the *Song of Hastings*, which bluntly observes, 'And blazing from heaven the streaming hair of the comet proclaimed to the English foreordained destruction.'[17]

The last of the scenes centred around Westminster shows the recently crowned Harold being informed about the appearance of the comet. The episode is located in a palace which is a more elaborate structure than that portrayed in the previous scene. It has a turret staircase and a spiral column embroidered in two colours. Two storeys are shown with one pepper-pot dormer on the roof, which is tiled.

There are two birds on the roof, whose appearance might have been intended as an ill omen. Harold is still sitting on the throne, holding a lance, and is bending his head and body towards a messenger who is carrying a sword. Harold's whole demeanour is entirely different from when he appeared in the acclamation scene. He appears to be deeply concerned and no longer carries the hauteur of kingship. The drama of this scene is heightened by the depiction of the outline of five ships at sea in the border immediately below; they are not armed and carry no crew.

Various attempts have been made to link these vessels with events in the first half of 1066, but there seems little doubt that the appearance of the ghostly armada is a premonition of the Norman invasion in September. The caption, 'Harold', tells us nothing more than that the English king was at the centre of this piece of theatre.

This scene of Harold's discomfort is linked by another contracted sea crossing to William's court on the other side of the Channel. There is no indication where the vessel sailed from or where it landed in France; the depiction of the passage is abbreviated at either end by a single tree on the water's edge. Like Harold the duke is also seated within a palace, but unlike the new king, who is alone apart from a messenger, William has advisors around him. The Norman group is very animated, presumably reacting to the news that Harold has been crowned.

Chapter 7

Duke William Prepares for War

fter the arrival of the vessel bearing the unwelcome news of Harold's accession to the throne, the tempo of the Tapestry speeds up.

Duke William, in the company of Bishop Odo, receives the news of what he regards as Harold's duplicity and on the advice of the bishop immediately orders the building of an invasion fleet. The scene takes place in a ducal palace, probably in Rouen, although it has been suggested that it could have been at Fécamp or Lillebonne (Seine-Maritime), one of William's palaces which survived largely intact until the nineteenth century.

The palace depicted on the Tapestry has two turrets on the left-hand side and one on the right. All three are capped by conical domes, and sloping shingle roofs suggest the presence of attached buildings of unknown character. In the centre of the bow-shaped roof there is another little pepper-pot turret, sitting on a rectangular bed of a shingled roof. Duke William is shown, without any insignia or indicators of rank, sitting on a throne which has carved animal heads at the ends of the armrests. On his right is a clergyman, almost certainly his half-brother Bishop Odo of Bayeux. Although Odo seems to be seated a little behind the duke, the body language of the scene clearly shows that the bishop is directing the conversation. The text states, 'Here Duke William ordered ships to be built' but it is Odo who is

Bayeux Tapestry. News of Harold's coronation is taken across the English Channel by a ship carrying eight men, with shields along the bows.

Bayeux Tapestry. Duke William seated on a throne with his half-brother Odo receives the news from England. They order the building of an invasion fleet.

giving the orders to a carpenter holding an adze standing beside him. This is the bishop's first appearance in the Tapestry and here, as in the other scenes in which he features, he is shown to be in command and leading events. Such depictions of Odo playing a decisive role appear at critical stages of the story and are one of the main reasons why the bishop is believed to have been involved in the creation of the Tapestry.

The Romanesque ducal palace at Lillebonne, Seine Maritime, which was destroyed in the nineteenth century. It might have been built from material taken from the ruins of the Roman town of *Juliobona*; the medieval town walls were built of re-used Roman masonry and bricks.

Woodsmen are shown felling trees, and carpenters and shipwrights construct the vessels that will carry the French army to England. This is followed by the collection of arms and provisions immediately before William and his men embark for the invasion.

This section of the hanging is particularly important as it contains images of armour, weaponry and items of food and drink and also emphasizes the care that went into planning the Norman armada. It effectively telescopes the activities of William and the Normans between January and September 1066 into four scenes, but the Tapestry manages to convey the urgency and the energy that went into these preparations. The Tapestry designer was concerned to evoke the scale of the task of creating the invasion fleet. This activity together with the other arrangements would have involved a large number of Normans in the war effort; according to William of Poitiers, 'Almost all of Normandy was devoted to the task.' The sight of such urgent industry would in itself have reinforced the propaganda that William would have been employing to emphasize the importance of the forthcoming mission. Wace wrote:

You would have witnessed building materials and wood being brought energetically to all the ports throughout Normandy, pegs being made and edges trimmed, ships and skiffs prepared, sails raised and masts put up. With great effort and at great cost, the whole of one summer and one August they spent getting the ships ready and assembling the troops.[1]

In addition, councils were assembled and missions despatched in order to persuade Norman and other barons to support William. No doubt other forms of inducement including bribery would have been used both within and outside the duchy. These diplomatic projects eventually resulted in the formation of the alliance that was to create William's military forces at Hastings, but evidence of all this diplomatic activity is absent from the Tapestry.

The gathering of an invasion force was a mighty effort that went beyond assembling the soldiers and creating a fleet, critical as these were. William's army used hundreds of horses that needed to be trained and cared for. Additionally, there would have been a small army of non-combatants to accompany the fighting men – cooks, bakers, carpenters, blacksmiths, farriers, ostlers, servants and clergy.

Many parts of Normandy would have been involved in the war effort, but the Tapestry gives few clues as to where these preparations that it portrays took place. The estuarine bays of Lower Normandy would have been particularly busy, as would the river ports and forests along the Seine, with Rouen as a location where much ship construction would have taken place. There is a suggestion in a document of 1035 that the port of Harfleur at the mouth of the Seine might already have been in use as a Norman naval base. William of Jumièges reported that a Norman ducal navy had existed in the time of William's father, Robert I, who in 1033–34 had assembled a fleet ostensibly with the purpose of reinstating Edward (the Confessor) and his brother, Alfred, in England.

At this stage, the Tapestry wants to convey the message that the whole of Normandy was participating in the invasion preparations and the precise geographical locations involved did not need to be referenced. Nevertheless, the Tapestry does portray both coastal and woodland landscapes as well as buildings as background to the events leading up to war.

Building the Invasion Fleet

Bishop Odo and a carpenter standing next to him are inside the palace, pointing outwards to three foresters with axes cutting down trees.

This scene marks the start of a flurry of activity preparing for the invasion, starting with the building of a fleet of Viking-style boats. The fleet is represented by the hulls of five completed ships and two boats which are in the process of construction. The Tapestry implies that the fleet, which was initially gathered together at Dives-sur-Mer in Lower Normandy in August 1066, was built from scratch. In reality, many of the ships which sailed to England would have been donated or appropriated as ready-functioning vessels.

The duke would already have had some of these in his possession as part of the Norman navy. Others would have been requisitioned from subordinate lords on the basis of a levy, similar to the Scandinavian *leidhangr* or English knight's

Bayeux Tapestry. Woodmen cutting trees into planks for the invasion fleet.

A modern wreck on the shore behind the estuarine spit at Dives-sur-Mer, where the invasion fleet gathered initially.

service, where individuals were required to supply services or goods to their lord in return for protection. In England, ships were commandeered on several critical occasions during Edward the Confessor's reign.

It is not certain how many ships were used by William in the invasion; a twelfth-century ship list suggests that 776 vessels were supplied by fourteen of Normandy's leading barons. Amongst these was Bishop Odo, who contributed 100 ships, and his brother, Robert of Mortain, who is recorded as providing the largest number with 120 vessels. The document also claims that William actually had 1000 vessels at his disposal; the discrepancy in numbers might be accounted for by William's own contribution to the force.[2] Other chroniclers postulate widely differing numbers of ships involved, ranging from Wace's 696 ships to Gaimar's improbable 11,000. It is futile to attempt to ascertain the precise number of vessels in the fleet as it is unlikely that they were ever systematically counted at the time and, even if they were, no reliable documentary record survives.[3]

The Tapestry shows the transformation of trees into planks for use in the new boats. Some scholars have argued that the magnates who were assigned ship quotas built them from the forests on their lands. On the other hand, Wace stated that ships were constructed in the various ports of Normandy. Undoubtedly, the shipyards of Rouen would have figured prominently in the war effort. Not only was Rouen a major trading port, it was at the centre of a group of ducal forests. There was extensive woodland on either side of the River Seine, dating back at least to

Bayeux Tapestry. Workmen building boats before the invasion.

Carolingian times. On the right bank lay the forests of Lillebonne, Maulévrier, Jumièges, Roumare, Selvoisson (now la Forêt Verte), Longboël (which extended north-eastwards to the forest of Lyons), Les Andelys and Vernon; while on the left bank lay those of Brotonne, Vatteville, Mauny, Rouvray, Londe, Bord and Bizy.[4] The Seine Valley forests must have provided the lion's share of the timber used in building new ships for the invasion fleet.

The ships that were built would have supplemented those seaworthy vessels already in Norman ports. The use of timber from freshly felled trees would only have taken place after the stores of seasoned timber in port facilities had been exhausted. This wood was readily accessible for use and involved no transportation costs. Nonetheless, the shipwrights appear to have been compelled to build some vessels from unseasoned green timber. Viking shipbuilders are known to have built their vessels from wood that was seasoned through immersion in seawater, although they did use green wood on occasion. The trees depicted in the boatbuilding scenes have tall, straight trunks without irregularities; they are also notably thinner and straighter than those depicted elsewhere in the Tapestry.

Baudri de Bourgueil wrote that William issued an 'imperial edict' ordering his magnates to undertake the construction of some of the ships that were needed to invade England. Baudri's poem provides valuable details of the ships and the way they were constructed.[5] He writes that William commanded that the ships should be completed by 5 May 1066, just four months after he ordered their construction. Baudri then explained that those men responsible for providing the *naves* oversaw the cutting down of huge numbers of trees. Baudri next describes the building and fitting of the ships in some detail:

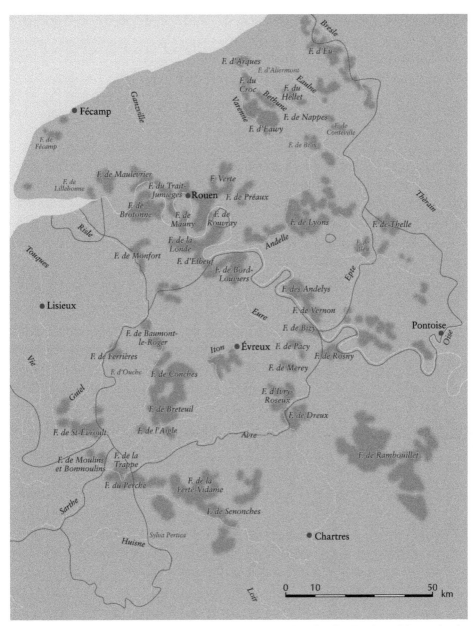

Map of the Norman dioceses of Rouen and Evreux showing the distribution of forests in the eleventh century (after Baudwin 2004, 46).

Bilge-holds, oars, sailyards, cross-banks, yardropes,
and other items of use are fitted by everyone.
Forests are cut down – the ash, the oak, and the ilex fall;
the pine is uprooted by the trunk.
The aged fir is hauled down from the steep mountains;
labour gives value to all trees.

He claimed that the trees used in building the ships were ash, oak, holm oak, pine and silver fir. As three of these species were not found in Normandy, Baudri seems to have been applying poetic licence. It is, however, generally agreed that oak and pine were the main timbers used in the construction of northern European boats at the time.

Baudri's account mirrors the pictorial narrative of the Tapestry, where the building and outfitting of the ships is portrayed carefully. As was usual with these clinker-built vessels, the keel and stern posts were laid first. The shell was then created and the frames carved to fit. Finally, the oar-ports were made and detachable figureheads were fitted fore and aft. During the course of construction the ship was secured by a series of stakes. On the Tapestry, following the felling of trees and the lopping of branches, a workman uses an adze to plane a plank that has been wedged into the fork of the stump of a tree. He is surrounded by finished planks ready for use.

The Tapestry suggests that the preparation of the timber for building took place close to where the trees were chopped down, but it is more likely to have been undertaken at the shipyard, where the finished timbers were assembled to create the hulls. Some scholars have suggested that the piles of wooden planks seen around the woodsman on the Tapestry do show that large logs were split in the forest and were then transported to the shipyard, where they were squared and finished.[6]

Bayeux Tapestry. Weapons, armour and supplies of food being taken to the invasion ships.

On the Tapestry, the woodsmen are using a variety of tools, including light felling axes to lop off suitable branches from the trees. They employ T-shaped axes to square off a balk (a rough timber beam) and to give a final trim to an already fastened strake, and a small hand-axe is used to trim planking. Both breast augers and T-handled augers are shown in use to bore holes. It has been suggested that an ill-defined tool in the right hand of one of the shipwrights could be a shave to finish off a plank or possibly an early form of bevel gauge, used to check that the correct angle has been worked along the top edge of a plank so that the next strake can be fitted at the required angle.[7] In addition to the tools mentioned above, the craftsmen depicted on the Tapestry use straight-blade axes, hammers and side axes. Such implements have been found in contemporary maritime late Saxon and Viking archaeological contexts.[8] The construction of both the Graveney boat (tenth century) and the Skuldelev wrecks (eleventh century) shows that the shipwrights almost always used axes in preference to saws.

Once the backbone of the boat was in place, a start was made on planking the hull. Planks were made from radially split oak trunks or from tangentially split softwood trees. The first strake was fastened to the underside of the keel flange. A strake is a run of planking from one end of the vessel to the other, which might be made up of several planks scarfed together. The plank ends were tapered to a feather edge so that when they overlapped at the scarfs there was no increase in the thickness of the strake. Caulking (waterproofing material) was put between the strake edges and into the scarfs as they were assembled. This was made of animal hair or moss, generally mixed with tar. Contemporary samples of animal hair which have been analysed, from Dublin and London, show that cow or horse hair was used, probably the by-products of the tanning industry. A sample of sheep's wool, from London, had been dyed, indicating that it was probably textile waste. At the Queen Street waterfront in Newcastle, seventy-three small, twisted rolls and flattened pads of fibre were identified as caulking material from clinker-built vessels. Of the twenty-five samples examined for species analysis, thirteen were of cattle hair and ten of sheep's wool with two possible examples of goat hair.

The edges of the strakes and the scarfs were fastened with iron clench nails. These nails had large, round heads and were hammered from outboard to inboard through partly pre-bored holes. On the inboard face of the planking, the shanks were hammered over and clenched against quadrilateral roves. The extreme ends of the strakes were feathered for fastening to the stern and stern posts with iron spike nails. The hull planking was built up as a shell, probably largely by eye. Levels and width gauges might be used to make the shapes of the two sides of the hull as similar as possible, but exact symmetry was rarely achieved.[9]

Boat building was a specialized profession and in Scandinavia there seems to have been a distinction between two groups of workmen involved in the construction of warships, and this difference may be shown among the shipworkers on the Tapestry.[10] The final stage of fitting out the ships was completed by experienced craftsmen, identified as such on the Tapestry by their beards, compared to the clean-shaven younger men involved in the earlier stages of the work. One of the men, probably a master boat builder, standing in front of the stern of a partly built boat is checking the work of the carpenters to confirm that the boat's lines were fair.[11]

As soon as they were built, the ships were launched without masts. The caption on the Tapestry reads, 'Here they drag the ships to the sea.'

Five men are shown hauling two vessels off the beach into shallow water. They appear to be using a pulley attached to a single dock post or piling standing in the water. This device is capped by a crown-like decoration on top of which stands one of the border birds. There are three other ships ready for launching, two of which already have forward figureheads attached.

The next scene shows other preparations for the invasion, with the transfer of military armour and weaponry and provisions towards the fleet. In addition to weapons and food supplies, the invading army would have needed to take tents, bedding and containers for storing and preparing food. This episode is divided from the shipbuilding scenes by a simple building with three tall arches under a pitched, tiled roof. The building may have been a decorative device, but it is surrounded by waves and has footings sitting on the shore. It could, therefore, also represent a port building.

There is little information available on the specific details of the preparations for the invasion and we do not know where these scenes on the Tapestry are located. It is possible that some of the fleet was built at the mouth of the River Touques, near the ducal castle at Bonneville, which lay close to the forest of Touques (St Gatien), but it is known that the main rendezvous for the ducal fleet was further west at Dives-sur-Mer, at the mouth of the River Dives. The evidence from medieval

Bayeux Tapestry. The invasion ships are taken to the water.

salt production sites shows that the estuarine lagoon here was much larger in the Middle Ages than it is now.

Significantly, there was already a Norman whaling fleet, under the control of the ducal abbey of Fécamp, based at Dives-sur-Mer, which could well have provided an important source of shipping for the invasion.[12] Normans, Flemings and Basques were involved in whaling, which had perhaps been introduced to the region by the Vikings. It appears that the whales which were hunted in the North Sea, English Channel and Bay of Biscay belonged to a variety called the Biscayan or black whale. This was a type of whale that was hunted virtually to extinction in the later Middle Ages. Although contemporary references to whaling are rare, in the eighth century the abbey of St Denis had been granted the hunting concession off the Cotentin Peninsula, and a Corporation for Whaling, 'wallmanni', was established in Normandy in 1098. There are also eleventh-century references to the trading of whale meat at Arras, Nieuwpoort, Calais and Boulogne.[13] Ralph Tortaire, writing of the Calvados coastal area in the early twelfth century, noted that, 'In winter time they take whales.'[14] The relevance of whaling to William's invasion fleet was that this form of hunting required a significant number of ships to succeed. Whaling fleets must have been relatively large and in this case would have been able to provide the duke with a considerable number of ready-built ocean-going vessels, the presence of which at Dives could well have determined his choice of assembly port.

The task of gathering a large army together in one place and maintaining it over several months was a formidable one. In the summer of 1066, Harold's English army quartered with his fleet along the south coast and on the Isle of Wight, but it appears that the available supplies were so depleted that by early September it was necessary to demobilize all his military resources. The *Anglo-Saxon Chronicle* records that, 'Then when it was the Nativity of St Mary (8 September), the men's provisions were gone, and no one could hold them there any longer.' Meanwhile, in Normandy, according to William of Poitiers, Duke William was faced with a similar problem, but dealt with it more systematically by paying his troops on a regular basis and strictly forbidding plunder and looting.

The area around Dives had good communications with other parts of Normandy, which would have been essential to establish and maintain a military encampment for several weeks before embarkation; according to one estimate such a base would have had to accommodate up to 14,000 men and 2000–3000 horses.[15] There would have needed to be a highly structured and closely co-ordinated process by which the duke's agents obtained the required supplies through a wide variety of purchases and requisitions. To some extent, Duke William was able to rely on supplies kept in a number of depots where '*le foin de roi*' was gathered. For some items of equipment, such as spears, arrows, replacement weapons, armour and some food items such as wine and salt pork, his army would have been totally dependent on depots. Even for fodder for the horses, the depots would have helped

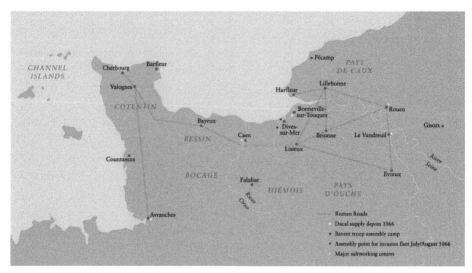

Plan of ducal depots and Roman roads in Normandy.

to ensure a regular supply. It is estimated that a horse required 5 kilos (10lb) of hay per day just for maintenance, plus at least 36 litres (8 gallons) of water a day. There were five ducal depots in Normandy, at Caen, Avranches, Bonneville-sur-Touques, Rouen and Le Vaudreuil. These were important ducal residences and the depots would have maintained the ducal cavalry and the ducal hunt, but they would also have played an essential role in the military preparations of 1066.[16]

The Gulf of Dives was one of the most important salt-producing areas in Normandy in the early Middle Ages and was well served by a network of dedicated salt roads connecting coastal salt pans with Caen, Falaise and Rouen. Although it is not certain where the waiting troops were located precisely, traces of eleventh-century occupation found at Bavent, a few kilometres to the south-west of Dives next to Varaville, appear to mark the location of a military holding camp.[17] The chronicler Wace observed that the Dives flowed into the sea near Bavent, which now lies almost 5km from the coast.

The Norman Cavalry

Many observers have commented on the importance of horses in William's victory at Hastings. The stabling, feeding and watering in Normandy, as well as the transport of a large number of cavalry horses to England, was a logistical triumph. The Tapestry lays great stress on the quantity and splendour of the Norman warhorses, which were called destriers, or Great Horses. It seems likely that the modern draft breed of Percheron is partly descended from the Norman warhorse. Recent research on medieval warhorses suggests that they averaged 14–15 hands and differed from a riding horse in their strength, musculature and training, rather than their size.[18] It appears that part of the attraction to mercenaries joining the Norman forces was the large number of warhorses the duke had at his disposal. These horses fetched high prices and were commonly used as part-payment for grants of land. Horse-breeding was linked to the increasingly well-endowed monasteries, for example, Jumièges. It seems probable that the Normans only transported warhorses across the Channel and requisitioned packhorses and riding horses when they arrived in England. The Normans had acquired Spanish horses as gifts through their early involvement in the reconquest of Spain. The Normans in southern Italy and Sicily would also have encountered Barbary and Arabian horses, some of which would have found their way north to Normandy. It was claimed that 'the great men of Gascony and the Auvergne' and 'likewise the kings of Spain' sought Duke William's friendship with gifts of horses. Reputedly, the horse ridden by William at Hastings had been brought from Spain by William Giffard, who accompanied the duke to England. There has been considerable discussion about the way in which the Norman horses were transported to England. Some observers suggested that they were suspended in hammocks to avoid them falling over during the voyage.[19] Others believe that the horses were carried on open-deck longships, which on arrival in England were tipped over on the beach to allow the animals to step over the gunwales. The depiction of the arrival at Pevensey on the Tapestry suggests that this is what the designer was trying to portray.

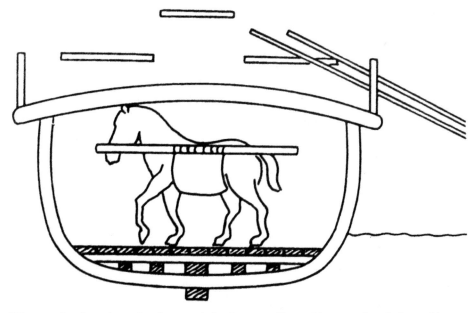

Diagram showing a horse in a hammock for the cross Channel journey. A technique of horse-transport developed by Arab mariners in the Mediterranean and adopted by Normans in Italy.

Armour and Weaponry

The Tapestry shows suits of armour being carried to the ships. The main body protection was called the hauberk, a leather shirt to which riveted metal rings were sewn. This was worn mainly by the cavalry. It was in the form of a long mail shirt, split at the groin, with flaps hanging down from the thighs to the knees. On the Tapestry, the hauberk is shown with short sleeves and occasionally a separate mail forearm protection extending from under the hauberk sleeve down to the wrist. During the battle scenes, some of the soldiers are shown with mail leggings, but none of the figures on the Tapestry have any protection of hands or feet.

The Norman shields were kite-shaped with rounded tops. They were made of wood with an iron boss and probably with iron bands around the edge. In addition, the Tapestry shows straight-bladed longswords, lances, a battleaxe and helmets being carried to be loaded. The longswords, which were used by both armies, weighed 1–2k (2lb 4oz–4lb 8oz) and had pommels, grips and hand-guards. The lances were about 2m (6ft 6in) long and made of wood with triangular, tipped metal blades. Battleaxes were only used by the English housecarls in the battle scenes, but a single axe is being carried to the waiting Norman ships. This would have been a Danish axe, consisting of a wooden handle and a solid iron head weighing up to 3k (6lb 12oz). The helmets were made of soldered metal plates and were conical in shape with a nasal protection. There are no bows in view, but on top of the cart carrying a large barrel there are dozens of arrows. In battle two types of weapon are shown; short bows fixed at chest height and longbows fired from the jaw.

Saint-Valery-sur-Somme

The invasion fleet appears to have moved from the Dives estuary in Normandy to the Somme estuary in Ponthieu at some time in August 1066. It is possible that essential supplies in Lower Normandy had been exhausted or that William had planned all along to move his army closer to England for the final invasion. The Tapestry ignores the activities of the fleet before its departure for England, but the *Carmen de Hastingae Proelio* (c.1067) opens with the movement of the fleet to Saint-Valery-sur-Somme. It describes how the weather was tempestuous, rainy and cold, and responsible for driving the fleet 'willy-nilly' to Saint-Valery. The Norman fleet suffered a number of lost ships during the transfer and William of Poitiers explains how the duke buried the evidence of the disaster in order not to discourage his troops.

There is a small walled town at Saint-Valery, parts of whose defensive circuit may date from before the Conquest. The *Carmen* describes the inhabitants of the estuarine town as 'skilled in war, always faithful and often offering refuge to the shipwrecked'. The town sits on the southern bank of the Somme estuary, which has been heavily silted since Norman times.

Medieval gateway to the walled town of St Valery-sur-Somme, from whence the invasion fleet sailed.

In the eleventh century, the town probably lay on a promontory, almost surrounded by water. The church contained the relics of the seventh-century St Valery. William ordered the bones of St Valery to be taken out of the church and carried in a solemn procession around the town walls, during which the saint was called upon to intercede with God to provide a favourable wind. It is said that on 27 September the wind changed and there was a rush to board the fleet in order to sail on the evening tide. Saint-Valery has an enormous tidal reach of up to 9.5 miles.

Chapter 8

The Invasion

Thehe next section of the Tapestry shows the Norman invasion fleet sailing to England and events on the south coast in the prelude to the Battle of Hastings. The Norman fleet set sail from Saint-Valery-sur-Somme on the evening of 27 September 1066. Just three days earlier, King Harold had achieved a decisive victory over a Scandinavian army at Stamford Bridge in Yorkshire. In mid September, Harold's half-brother Tostig, in alliance with King Harald Hardrada of Norway, attacked York. Harald III of Norway is one of the most interesting eleventh-century figures and is often described as the last of the Viking chieftains. He had been wounded at the Battle of Stiklestad (1030), in which his half-brother St Olaf was killed, but had escaped to serve as a mercenary soldier in Kiev. He then went on to join the Byzantine emperor's Varangian guard in Constantinople. He later returned to Norway and successfully contended for the crown of Norway, where his strong rule earned him the sobriquet 'Hardrada' or 'hard counsel' (1046–66).

On the death of Edward the Confessor, Harald believed that he had a claim to the English throne and raised a large army to invade England. He joined forces with Tostig in September and decisively defeated the English northern earls Edwin and Morcar at the Battle of Gate Fulford (20 September). Hearing the news of the English defeat, King Harold reassembled his army and marched swiftly northwards. On 25 September, he surprised and overwhelmed the invaders at the Battle of Stamford Bridge, where both Harold Hardrada and Tostig were killed. One source at least suggests that Harold used both mounted troops and archers at Stamford Bridge for both advance and pursuit. According to the *Heimskringla* (The Lives of the Norse Kings), *c*.1230, 'the English rode upon them from all sides and threw spears and shot at them'. Another account speaks of the battle ending when Harald was killed by an arrow which hit him in the throat. It was reported that of the 300 ships that had transported the Norwegian army to England only 25 were required to carry the survivors home. Stamford Bridge was a great victory for the English and, undoubtedly, it is a battle which would have enjoyed a far higher historical profile had it not been for subsequent events in the south.

Stamford Bridge was also the last significant hand-to-hand battle to be fought on English soil; the Norman use of cavalry and bowmen was to change the face of English warfare for ever. So why, if the English cavalry had indeed been so effective at Stamford Bridge, were they not used at Hastings? The answer probably lies in Harold's haste to move south and challenge William.

Bayeux Tapestry. The fleet sails for Pevensey. Duke William's ship, the *Mora*, is in the centre foreground.

The Tapestry is silent about the English victory and about the subsequent forced march of over 340km (200 miles) that Harold and his troops were obliged to make southwards in order to confront William. The designer of the Tapestry is intent on conveying the drama of the Norman fleet crossing the Channel and the build-up to battle. The author needed to provide a smooth narrative uninterrupted by what would have been perceived as the unnecessary ambiguity of Harold's great victory. The Tapestry clearly had no interest in celebrating Harold's military prowess against another enemy in the north or providing evidence of mitigating factors to account for the eventual English defeat.

Although it is 120km (75 miles) from Saint-Valery to Pevensey, the Tapestry shows the Channel crossing in the form of a continuous line of ships stretching from the French to the English shore.

Bayeux Tapestry. The fleet arrives in England and the horses are unloaded.

Nine ships are shown in the foreground and three in the background. The ships are demonstrably seen to be in motion, their sails spread before the southerly wind William had prayed for and straining at their ropes. The impression of a crowded sea is given by the boats jostling close to each other. Six of the boats are carrying horses and all of them have their masts raised and sails set; no oars are used during the voyage. The ship approaching the English shore is being manoeuvred with a pole, its mast is being lowered and its horses disembarked immediately before it is dragged up on to the beach. Eight of the ships have a helmsman operating a rudder as well as handling the sails. There is no evidence of the weapons or supplies which had been loaded in the previous scenes. Several of the ships have figureheads of the usual Scandinavian design, but these are missing from those ships drawn up on the beach.

The fifth ship from the left is the *Mora*, William's own vessel. It has a distinctive figurehead described below and at the stern is a small human figure carrying a short lance and pennant in its left hand and blowing a horn held in its right. This striking feature was known to contemporary Normans and according to the *Brevis Relatio*, written at Battle Abbey about fifty years afterwards, the prow of the duke's ship was carved in the form of 'a little golden boy pointing to England with his right hand, and holding an ivory horn to his mouth with his left'.[1] Wace reported that the prow on the duke's ship was decorated with a copper image of a boy armed with a drawn bow and arrow pointed towards England. The duke's vessel is also distinguished by a crossed square with another cross on top sited at the masthead. This has sometimes been incorrectly interpreted as the papal banner given to William by Pope Alexander II. The explanation is probably more prosaic and the image is of a lantern designed to help the fleet stay together during the night's voyage. The Tapestry text states that, 'Here Duke William in a great ship crossed the sea and came to Pevensey.' It has been estimated that the fleet would have set sail from France at about 5.30 pm and arrived at Pevensey Bay at about 9.00 am the following morning.

Baudri noted:

Moreover, there were separate ships for the infantry;
some ships carried the cavalry; others, the horses.

And that:

And now the steersman watches the wind and the stars,
and the men immediately fall to their tasks.
Turning the folds of their sails, they veer into the wind.
At length their oars fall silent and they gain the shore.

Medieval drawing of Duke William falling on disembarkation in England. This was seen as a bad omen by the Normans, but the duke claimed that he had 'grasped' English soil.

On the Tapestry, the end of the voyage is signified by a group of empty hulls drawn up almost in parallel at the water's edge. Apart from unloading two horses, no attempt is made to show the disembarkation of men or supplies. This activity is implied by the empty boats on the shore.

Immediately afterwards, two cavalrymen holding shields and lances are shown riding at evident speed away from the fleet, thus transferring the momentum of the Tapestry from sea to land. Before that, the horses were unloaded from a ship whose mast was being lowered. They appear to be stepping over the side of the boat that had carried them from France. It is more likely that wooden ramps would have been set up to help them off the vessels. This would have been the first time that William had ferried horses, but the Normans in the Mediterranean already had experience of transporting horses by water. In 1061 the Norman Robert Guiscard (Duke of Sicily 1059–85) had taken horses from southern Italy for an attack on Muslim Sicily. In this instance, he seems to have used specially designed horse transport ships, which could each carry twenty-one animals. No such specialized transport seems to have been available to Duke William.

The anchor which is being carried ashore from one of William's ships appears to be similar in form and size to one found at Ladby, Denmark, dating to around AD 900. The anchor's arms end in 'flukes', a shaping of the ends to increase holding power. Like the Ladby anchor, this one also has a ring at the crown as well as an anchor ring to which a cable of unknown material is fastened.[2]

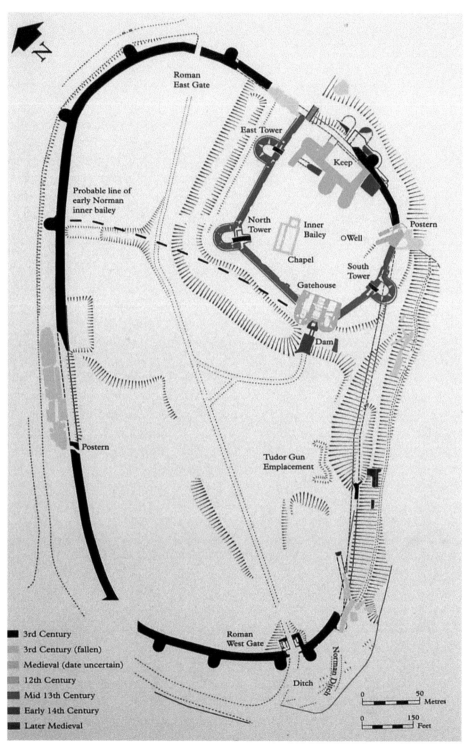

Plan of Saxon Shore fort at Pevensey dating from the third century, where the Norman troops encamped after crossing the Channel. Pevensey is specifically named on the Tapestry.

Aerial view of the Saxon Shore fort at Pevensey. In 1066 the sea would have surrounded the area of the peninsula – on which the fort sits.

Pevensey

'Thus with a favourable wind, they all reached Pevensey, and there without opposition they disembarked.' William of Poitiers thus confirms the Tapestry's depiction of the invasion force landing at Pevensey. He added, 'Rejoicing greatly at having secured a safe landing, the Normans seized and fortified Pevensey and then Hastings.'

The Norman ships landed close to the Roman fortifications at Pevensey Castle (*Anderitum*). It is difficult to believe that William landed here by accident; if he did, it was great good fortune for him. It was a heavily defended walled enclosure, which would have given protection to much of his army. It had earlier been garrisoned by Harold's men before they had dispersed, but there was no opposition waiting for the Norman forces and they were able to dig in without any hindrance. The south coast had been guarded by soldiers on land and patrolled by the Saxon navy until the late summer of 1066. Harold's forces were then disbanded, partly because of a shortage of supplies, partly because it was believed that the threat from William had passed for the time being, but more urgently because there was the threat of a Scandinavian invasion in the north-east of England.

The Norman fleet landed in what was then a much larger bay than is evident today. The geography of the coastline on which it landed has changed dramatically over the last millennium. Several watercourses flowed into Pevensey Bay and then into the sea, having passed through the low-lying marshy area now known as the Pevensey Levels. The levels were open water in Roman times and the distribution of dozens of salt works in what are now inland areas recorded in Domesday Book shows that tidal water still covered much of the area in the eleventh century. References to Pevensey during the eleventh century are normally linked to ships taking refuge in a harbour there. There has been a great deal of drainage, canalization and river diversion as well as woodland clearance in the surrounding Weald, which has resulted in the silting up of Pevensey Bay. Consequently, *Anderitum*, which originally lay on a narrow peninsula at the mouth of the bay in 1066, is now separated from the sea by a swathe of marshland about 1.4km (1 mile) wide.

Roman *Anderitum* had originally been built to defend the south coast against the Anglo-Saxons in the third century AD as one of a string of fortifications on either side of the Channel, known as the forts of the Saxon Shore. The Pevensey fort

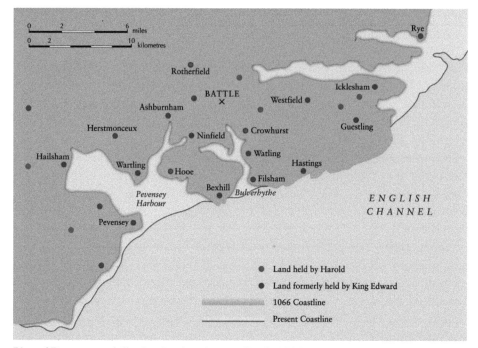

Plan of Pevensey and district showing the coastline in 1066 and the estates held by Harold in the vicinity of Pevensey and Hastings.

enclosed an area of over 3 hectares (*c*.8 acres) and the original walls, still standing to a height of up to 6m (20ft) in places, were strengthened by a series of round towers. On landing, William reinforced the existing fortifications by narrowing the former Roman west gate with a wall in front of the guard chambers and cutting away a curving ditch in front. The arch of the Roman east gate was also repaired and fighting platforms were added to two other towers. A pit containing a wooden ladder, a cask, bowls and four eleventh-century jugs from Normandy has been excavated in the outer bailey, and it is thought that these objects belonged to the invading force. After the Conquest, Pevensey was granted to Robert of Mortain, William's other half-brother. He founded a small borough outside the Roman fort, repairing the original walls and building a castle within it.

The conventional story told by the chroniclers is that after landing at Pevensey, William built a castle. The next day he moved his fleet and troops eastwards to Hastings, where he built a second castle. Yet topographically this is distinctly odd. Saxon Hastings was little more than a small fishing village, which is not recorded in Domesday Book, with a harbour that appears on the face of it to have been inadequate to accommodate a fleet the size of William's.

If Hastings had been a significant late Saxon port, it was not serving a populous hinterland. On the other hand, if the port of Hastings was serving long-distance inland trade, there should have been a network of roads leading from the town – no such routes, Roman or later, existed. Furthermore, virtually no Saxon coins or pottery have been found in the Hastings area. There is a remarkable lack of evidence for significant Saxon commercial activity immediately to the east of Pevensey Bay. The only suggestion of Saxon trading activity is provided by the place name Bulverhythe (OE: 'the landing place of the townspeople').[3] Some authors have suggested that Bulverhythe was in fact the site of Saxon Hastings, and that the place name indicated that this 'landing place' was serving a *burh*.[4] There is no harbour at Bulverhythe today, but historically the estuary of the Combe Haven stream was flooded inland as far as Wilting, just to the south of Crowhurst. There was a sandbank across the entrance to this bay, with two narrow channels on either side. The name of one of these openings survives as Glyne Gap. The ruins of St Mary's, a church founded by William of Eu in the late eleventh century, lie at the western end of the former sandbank.

It seems to have made little tactical sense to have moved from the safety of *Anderitum* and Pevensey Bay, with all its safe inlets, until such time that the army needed to move on. There was no coastal route from Pevensey to Hastings and William's army would have needed to circumnavigate the Pevensey Levels, a distance of approximately 25km (15.5miles). One intriguing suggestion that requires further investigation is that in the late Saxon period the place name 'Hastings' covered the whole region which included Pevensey and the later town of Hastings.[5] This area was occupied by the 'Haestingas', a group of Saxons that remained isolated from the rest of Sussex. They mainly settled the coastal margins, particularly at the heads of the then several river valleys which were inlets of the sea south of the upland known as Battle Ridge. It may also be significant that the Romans called the Weald the Forest of Andred after *Anderitum,* from which developed the Saxon name *Andredsweald* for the region. In 892 the *Anglo-Saxon Chronicle* had declared that the Wealden woodland was 'a hundred and twenty miles long or longer from east to west, and thirty miles broad'. The Wealden forest, which formed a barrier to the north of Hastings, was a region with a small population of scattered farms and hamlets, mainly used as common wood pasture by larger settlements around its edge. During the eleventh century the Weald was still in the process of being settled.[6]

It could be argued that the name Pevensey was used in connection with the bay and river rather than specifically with the fort at *Anderitum.* The use of the place-name suffix *ceastre* is invariably associated with Romano-British sites and there is no evidence of any significant Roman or Saxon occupation at Hastings. As many other Alfredian *burhs* were sited within former Roman fortifications, at places such as Winchester, Chichester and Portchester, it is possible that the place name *Haestingaceaster* was applied to the Roman fort at *Anderitum.* If this is the case, then William landed his fleet in Pevensey Bay on 28 September and moved his forces the short distance to *Anderitum* by land the following day. On the Tapestry, he is later seen supervising his troops building a castle at *Hestinga,* which could have been an earthwork constructed within the Roman fortifications. In logistical terms, this seems more likely than William moving his recently landed troops 25km to the east, around the difficult terrain of Pevensey Bay and across part of the Sussex Weald, possibly to a smaller harbour with less capacity than the one he was leaving.

The conventional argument used to support Hastings as the harbour to which William moved is that there has been significant coastal erosion here, which has removed all traces of the late Saxon port. In support of this idea is an early nineteenth-century drawing of the castle showing an area to the south of the present castle ruins known as the Gun, which has subsequently been eroded away.[7] The cliffs at Hastings are made up of the Ashdown and Wadhurst Formations of the Cretaceous era. These deposits consist of poorly cemented sandstones, silts, mudstones, pebble layers and clays, which are highly susceptible to erosion. The question of the presence or precise location of Hastings port and castle will remain a puzzle until there has been a thorough archaeological and topographical survey of the Hastings region.

It has been vigorously contended by one writer that the area around Lower Wilting Farm, near Crowhurst, was where William landed in 1066.[8] Although this suggestion is superficially attractive, there is no archaeological evidence to support it. Investigation ahead of the Bexhill to Hastings Link Road failed to identify any structural or artefactual evidence relating to the Norman invasion or the presence of a Saxon port here. Supposed evidence of putative boats and jetties at the Monkham Wood and Redgeland Wood inlets has been discounted as there is a discrepancy between the probable height of tidal waters in 1066 and the areas investigated as the location of boat finds and jetties. In 1066 mean sea level is likely to have been c.0.75m lower than at present, which means that it would have been impossible for the Normans to have landed here.[9]

The Tapestry makes no attempt to depict Pevensey or the coastal area where the Normans landed. Instead, it shows the two armed cavalrymen racing from the beached boats, with lances couched. This scene carries the text, 'And here the knights hurried to Hastings to get food.' The two knights are then seen guarding a foraging party who have collected a sheep, an ox and a pig. By this stage the Tapestry designer has stopped distinguishing the English from the Normans by their haircuts, but another source claims that the invaders' short, round Latin haircuts had actually led to a rumour being spread that William had landed with an army of monks.[10]

In the middle of this scene of foraging, apparently in charge, is a mounted knight specifically named on the Tapestry as Wadard, one of Bishop Odo's vassals. He appears to have been a provisions officer attached to the bishop's household and he was later rewarded with extensive estates in southern England. There are three single-storey houses in the background, presumably representing the Sussex farmsteads that were being raided. Two of them are built of horizontal boards, a design commonly found in the Scandinavian world – in Denmark they are known as *bulhns*. The first of the houses appears to have been built of stone as its walls are depicted with courses of rectangular blocks. This seems to be highly unlikely as the small number of eleventh-century vernacular houses that have been excavated have all been built with timber; added to which, the south Sussex Weald does not possess a good supply of natural building stone. It would appear that the designer

Bayeux Tapestry. Normans foraging for supplies in the Sussex countryside under the command of Wadard, one of Bishop Odo's vassals.

of the Tapestry is guilty of a flight of fancy, or simply wanted to use a different design from those on the other two houses. The first house also has an elaborate multicoloured roof which incorporates an area of wooden shingles, while the third has a tile or slate roof; all three roofs have finials at either end.

Sussex was at the heart of the Godwinsons' estates; about one third of the county was in their hands. Harold, who was probably a native of the county, held several large manors in the vicinity of Pevensey in his own right; these included Willingdon, Ratton, Hollington, Ninfield, Crowhurst and Hooe. As king, he also held Eastbourne, Jevingdon and part of Pevensey. Further east, Duke William appears to have had an interest in a number of estates around Rye which were probably held by the ducal monastery of Fécamp before the Conquest. In addition to part of the port of Rye itself, Fécamp held Winchelsea harbour, Brede, Bury and probably the extensive manor of Steyning which was assessed at 80 hides. While it can be assumed that the duke may have received safe haven on lands held by the Norman monastery, he would have been intent on causing as much damage as possible on his enemy's estates.

Although armies habitually foraged for their survival, the Normans' activities on King Harold's own land could well have precipitated his rapid return from the north and heightened his desire to engage with the enemy at the first opportunity. William of Poitiers observed that, 'The King [Harold] was the more furious because he had heard that the Normans had laid waste the neighbourhood of their

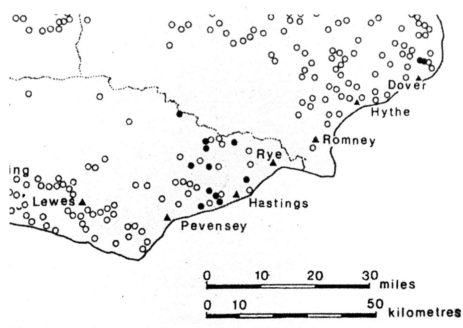

Waste (devastated) manors in Domesday Book (1086). Wholly waste estates are in black , partially waste open circles (After Derby H.C.)

Bayeux Tapestry. Preparing a feast before the Battle of Hastings.

camp.' These factors may well have been in Duke William's mind when choosing the ground for his operations. Here again, the Tapestry provides few clues as to precisely where the events occurred.

The next scene shows the Normans preparing and starting a meal. There are spitted chickens above a large cauldron hanging from a bar which is held by forked sticks over an open fire. At the same time, a white-bearded cook is using a long fork to take pies and cakes off a grill. The action is labelled, 'Here meat is cooked and here servants serve it.' Two servants, standing before a tall structure, are passing skewers and spitted fowl to a group of four men, presumably soldiers, at a makeshift table of long shields. One of them is holding a trumpet to his lips, perhaps giving the signal to start the meal.

To the right of the troops, there is a semicircular table surrounded by a group of Norman leaders. The scene is modelled on the iconographic tradition of the Last Supper and, significantly, Bishop Odo is seated at the head of the table in the place normally occupied by Christ. The caption explains, 'Here they have a meal and here the bishop blesses the food and drink.' Five other men are seated with him at the table, while a servant bearing a cup and a napkin curtseys before them. On the shield table are wooden bowls, bread and a knife, while on the bishop's there are, in addition to these items, fish and a miniature tripod 'cauldron'.

Comparisons have been drawn between Harold's feast at Bosham before his departure for Normandy and Odo's before the Battle of Hastings. They both take place before important events and both indicate the status of the diners.[11] There

Bayeux Tapestry. On the right Bishop Odo sits at the head of the table and blesses the meal; on the left soldiers take their meal off a makeshift table of shields.

The design of the feast on the Tapestry is based on a illustrations of the Last Supper found in contemporary and earlier illuminated manuscripts. (St Augustine's Gospels, Corpus Christi College MS.286.F.125R)

is one significant difference which has not received attention and that is that while the English banquet is located in a grand two-storey loggia, no attempt is made to indicate where the Normans were dining. There is no cobbling beneath the banqueting scene, suggesting that at least it was taking place indoors, but by this stage of the Tapestry the depiction of the ground surface has become erratic.

The Norman feasting scene is a crowded one, with the diners, a table full of food and drink, and a text which occupies all the space between the seated figures and the bottom of the upper frieze. It might be argued that there was no space for a building; however, to the left of the shield table there is a tall, narrow structure in the form of two towers and a banded roof. This could represent a hall or a portal to the building where the feast took place.

The next scene finds William seated between his two half-brothers in a council of war. They are portrayed within a simple wooden building with a triangular, shingled

Bayeux Tapestry. William and his half-brothers, Odo and Robert, confer before the Battle of Hastings.

roof. This is the only occasion on which the three brothers are shown together, and it is again Odo who is leading the discussions as William listens attentively. Robert is the man of action, drawing his sword and about to leave the council.

Once more there is no indication where this event took place, although the next caption states, 'The latter ordered that a castle should be dug at Hastings.' This caption appears over the scene showing a castle motte in the process of construction.

The chronicles do confirm that a second castle was constructed within days of the landing. It is mentioned not only by William of Jumièges and William of Poitiers, who records two castles, one at Pevensey and the other at Hastings, but also by the *Anglo-Saxon Chronicle*: 'Count William came from Normandy into Pevensey on the eve of Michaelmas and as soon as his men were able they constructed a fortification at the market of Hastings.' The workmen's shovels are rustic implements, relatively small and obviously easy to use, but perhaps not that

Bayeux Tapestry. Norman soldiers setting fire to a two-storey house from which a mother and child are escaping.

suitable for large-scale works. They are of a distinctively medieval and English design, made from wood except for a strip of metal, indicated by darker thread, to strengthen the digging edge; metal was expensive and in limited supply and hence would not be used for the entire blade. At the top of the shaft, these English shovels had an open handle for the hand to pass through, a feature also seen on German tools, but not on those used in France. They are also quite different from Scandinavian shovels, which were entirely wooden and did not have distinctive handles.

Immediately after the castle-building scene, the Tapestry shows a tower with a conical roof and steps leading to the entrance. This structure seems to have a seat, on which William is sitting, attached to it. The duke is receiving news of Harold's movements from a messenger, who is believed to be Vital, the cross-Channel merchant and Bishop Odo's vassal. The next scene is one of the most poignant in the whole Tapestry to modern eyes; a mother and her young son are shown escaping from a grand two-storey house which is being set alight by the Normans. The caption simply states, 'Here a house is burnt' – this is a disingenuous reference to the strategy of scorching the enemy's ground to make it uninhabitable.

King Harold Moves South

Despite their overwhelming victory at Stamford Bridge, King Harold and his army had suffered great losses in the battle, sapping their strength to counter the Norman invasion. The traditional story told is that Harold, seated at the formal banquet in York celebrating victory over the Scandinavians was brought, post-haste, a message to say that William had landed at Pevensey. On hearing of this second invasion, he gathered what forces he could muster and marched south in one of the most renowned forced marches in history.

Harold marched more than 320km (200 miles) in five or six days, arriving in London on 8 or 9 October. His force was much depleted, but would have included his housecarls and troops belonging to his brother Gyrth. Many of those who had fought at Stamford Bridge had been killed or wounded and he was hampered by a lack of vital supplies and transport. He also left behind the northern earls Edwin and Morcar, who had lost many men at the Battle of Fulford and whose task it was now to raise another northern army to fight the Normans.

After pausing in London for only five days, allowing him the minimum of time required to assemble what was effectively a new and untested army, Harold set out for the south coast. According to the *Anglo-Saxon Chronicle*, the king was advised by his mother and brother to wait until the arrival of the northern and western *fyrds*, but Harold was determined to attack the Normans at the earliest opportunity. His haste was probably partly due to overconfidence as a result of his victory at Stamford Bridge, and he would also have wanted to stop the damage to his homelands as quickly as possible.

Chapter 9

The Battle of Hastings

T he final surviving section of the Tapestry portrays the Battle of Hastings, starting with William being presented with his warhorse and ending with the death of Harold and the vanquished English troops leaving the battlefield. The battle scenes take up about one quarter of the entire work. With a few notable exceptions, no attention is given to the geographical features of the battlefield, but throughout most of the proceedings events take place on the wavy cobbling that is used to indicate the outdoor countryside.

Many of the battle scenes on the Tapestry are well known and over the years have been extensively used to illustrate textual histories of the Normans. Popular perceptions of Norman soldiers and of the death of Harold in particular are based on familiarity with their depiction on the Tapestry. Until recently the story and images of the battle as portrayed on the Tapestry have been accepted as reasonably accurate records of the events of 14 October 1066. Increasingly, however, scholars have questioned the authenticity of the Tapestry images and have been more critical of its account of the battle. Nonetheless, by vividly recreating the atmosphere of the battle through graphic representations of Norman warfare a credible impressionistic vision of what happened is created. Depictions of speed, violence and abrupt death all contribute to the veracity of the Tapestry's story.

The Battle

Numerically, the armies appear to have been well matched. Harold is thought to have had 6000 or 7000 men, although it is not known what the balance was between trained fighting men, thegns, housecarls and peasant militia. Duke William's army is thought to have consisted of some 2000 knights with 4000–5000 support troops. Their armour was almost identical, but their weapons and methods were different. The Saxons fought on foot with axes and javelins, whilst the Normans were able to employ cavalry, infantry and archers.

Before dusk on 13 October, Duke William heard that the enemy was within striking distance of his base at Hastings, and very early the following morning he moved his army northwards. Harold, confronted by the Normans, took up a defensive position along an escarpment known as 'the place of the grey apple tree' and to the Normans as 'Senlac' (sandy lake). Senlac Hill was the highest rise of ground between Hastings and the modern town of Battle. According to one source,

A medieval illustration of King Harold at the Battle of Stamford Bridge. (*Public Domain*)

the Normans, 'eager for battle', started to attack the Saxons well before their army was fully in position.

Much has been written about the Battle of Hastings, its tactics, and the relative qualities of the English and Norman troops and their commanders, but some aspects of this decisive conflict inevitably remain unclear. It is generally agreed that the Norman strategy was to sustain attacks up the short, steep incline to the summit of the hill on which Harold's shield wall was based. Their archers were able to weaken the English army, but in order to win it was necessary to penetrate Harold's ranks and destroy the elite forces of the wall in close combat. For much of the day the English repulsed the Norman attacks, and at times the Normans fell back in considerable confusion. At one point, the rumour spread that Duke William had been killed, and the Tapestry shows him lifting his helmet to show his face and thus reassure his troops. The Tapestry also portrays a number of Norman knights breaking through the English lines and the death of Harold's brothers Leofwine and Gyrth, long before the closing stages of the battle. As the day wore on, the Normans began to gain the advantage, partly by employing the tactic of the 'feigned flight', in which French contingents retreated in apparent confusion, tempting groups of English to pursue them down the hill. Careful drilling made it possible for the Norman cavalry then to turn in good order and charge down on the pursuing English infantry.

Eventually, the Normans penetrated through to the heart of the English command, where Harold still stood behind his shield wall with his dragon standard. The scene is vividly portrayed on the Tapestry; the standard was thrown down, the king's bodyguard was slaughtered, and Harold, wounded but still fighting, was cut down by a Norman knight. The Tapestry appears to show Harold with an arrow through his eye. This may have been a later alteration to the embroidery, but the Tapestry designer might also have invented this episode to underline the central theme of the narrative – God punishing the English and Harold in particular for his blind perjury. The Normans saw their success at the Battle of Hastings as a vindication of William's rightful claims to be the lawful successor to Edward the Confessor. Harold had received retribution as a disloyal vassal and was rightly overthrown.

The Battlefield

The site of the Battle of Hastings is an intrinsically improbable one. It is extremely unlikely that either army, given the choice, would have wanted to fight there. A remote location with appalling communications gave an advantage to neither side. William would surely have chosen a more open, less marshy landscape in which his cavalry could operate freely and Harold would have wished for a more secure site on which to plant his shield wall. It must have been an accident that brought the English and Norman armies together at what is now the town of Battle. One can imagine two armies struggling to locate each other in the woodland of the Weald and eventually having to make the best of a bad job. One of the reasons that the battle lasted so long, much longer than the usual few hours, was that neither side had been able to choose a site which gave them dominance.

Early English historians called the site of the battle Senlac, a name probably derived from the Old English word *sandache*, meaning a sandy place. Contemporary chroniclers call the battlefield 'the plain of Hastings', although the site is 11km north-west of the present town of Hastings and 15km from Pevensey. There has

Bayeux Tapestry. William is presented with a black stallion before the Battle of Hastings.

been considerable speculation about the precise movement of the two armies in the run-up to the battle and about the actual site of the battle. The consensus is that the fighting took place at the site now occupied by the town of Battle, between two hills, Caldbec Hill to the north and Telham Hill to the south. Battle town was created beside Battle Abbey, after the battle, in the late eleventh and early twelfth centuries. It is sited in the High Weald near the centre of the Battle Ridge, which extends south-eastwards from Hadlow Down (3km to the north-east of Uckfield) to meet the coast, where it forms dramatic cliffs at Fairlight (5km east of Hastings). The ridge consists of a succession of sandstones, siltstones and mudstones of the Hastings Beds (Lower Cretaceous). Clay ironstone provided ore for the Wealden iron industry from Roman Britain to the seventeenth century. The area was wooded and undulating, with patches of grassland and marsh resulting from the sluggish flow of the Wealden streams.

The isolated location of the battle site meant that reaching it from either direction would have been difficult, but Harold's route from the north would have been the most problematic. There are several routes that the English army could have taken to Battle. These include the line of a possible Roman road from Rochester to the Hastings area, used for the transport of Wealden iron, which has for long been favoured by local historians. There was another Roman road leading from London to Lewes, which Harold may have taken, but which would have involved marching on local tracks for the last few miles. The area is traversed with a network of trackways that served as livestock drove roads during the Middle Ages. It is unclear how these tracks originated as they appear to predate the Roman road system, but their deeply sunken and often muddy nature meant that they would not have provided easy access for either army.

There remains the question about precisely where in Battle was the battle fought? There have been many suggestions over time and in recent years there has grown an audience for conspiracy theories, that is, the belief that archaeologists and others are trying to hide the real site for reasons of professional pride.[1] This, of course, is nonsense; the problem is that the evidence is not strong enough to prove conclusively that the battle took place in any one place. The sloping ground immediately to the south-west of the Battle Abbey ruins has for long been the area favoured by many scholars and is now part of the English Heritage site at Battle. Topographically, it fits the description of a ridge, on which the abbey remains now sit, leading down to a stream, on the other side of which the ground rises. The assumption has been that the English occupied the ridge, while the Normans and their allies were lined up on the opposite slope. One of the arguments against this site has been that no archaeological remains from the battle have ever been recovered here. This can be countered by explaining that there would have been considerable soil slippage over a thousand years and that any material evidence is probably covered in several metres of silt and clay.

A recent Time Team examination of the site using LIDAR geophysics has raised further questions about the actual location of the battle. The survey indicated that the area conventionally believed to be the site of the battle, immediately to the south of Battle Abbey, would have been far too marshy for the repeated cavalry charges of the Normans. The survey also suggested that the ground to the east of Battle, along the A2100 road, was far firmer and that it was on this slope, leading to the town of Battle, that the battle was fought. On the face of it, the argument is a strong one and would simply involve moving the site by 90 degrees from its present assumed location. English Heritage insists that its site is where the battle occurred. The jury remains out on this issue, but new survey techniques may eventually come up with a convincing solution.[2]

The building depicted immediately before William is given his horse is the last portrayed on the Tapestry. The final quarter of the embroidery has no buildings and relatively few trees. It is true that there were no settlements in the region of Battle before the invasion and as such the Tapestry is accurate. The relative absence of trees is less credible as the Battle of Hastings took place in an area of semi-open woodland and marsh. The failure to depict either buildings or trees had more to do with the designer's need to create a rapid tempo for the battle scenes. Unlike the Breton campaign, which took the form of a series of interrupted sieges over several weeks, the Battle of Hastings took place in a single day. The structures and trees which were used in the Breton campaign helped to illustrate and explain the nature of the warfare. No such punctuation was required for the events of 14 October 1066. The designer believed that a minimum of landscape information was required, because the graphic unrolling battle itself created its own landscape.

Caldbec Hill near Battle, where the English army assembled before moving to the site of the Battle of Hastings.

The traditional site of the Battle of Hastings, with Battle Abbey in the background. A recent Lidar survey of the area has brought the authenticity of this site into question. It has been suggested that the ground at the foot of the slope would have been too wet to have been fought on and that the actual site is on the approach road from Hastings to Battle

Many of the details of military dress and weaponry shown on the Tapestry have been confirmed by archaeological finds of contemporary date found throughout Western Europe and Scandinavia. However, no systematic archaeological examination of the battlefield has taken place and only a very few artefacts from the conflict have been found. Among the rare finds is the head of a Saxon battleaxe which came to light during roadworks on Marley Lane in 1951; and it is now kept in Battle Museum.

The Armies Engage

Immediately after the burning of the town house on the Tapestry, a complex building is depicted, marking the change from the preparations to the battle itself. The building appears to be of three storeys and is flanked by a turret staircase; attached to it is a very large door hung on metal strap hinges. It has been suggested that this building represents the town of Hastings, as the caption adjacent to it states that, 'Here knights leave Hastings.'[3]

The main building has steps leading to it on either side, and on the outside on the ground in front of the building are five small roughly oval items, which

Bayeux Tapestry. The battle commences with the Norman cavalry couching their lances.

could be half-buried shields. Immediately to the right of the tower door, William stands, ramrod straight, bearing the same banner he was holding when previously he received news about Harold. The duke is then presented with a fine black stallion that is saddled and ready for action. From this point onwards, most of the characters depicted are armed.

Bayeux Tapestry. Although there is little attempt at depicting the landscape in which the battle was fought in this episode there is a low hill, which is used as a device to separate two similar scenes. In the first Duke William is asking the knight Vital if he has seen Harold, while in the second an unnamed soldier is warning King Harold of the approaching Norman army. This feature may have been used to indicate the undulating wooded Wealden landscape of low hills and valleys in the vicinity of Battle.

After the black horse scene, a group of three trees signal the start of the advance of the Norman cavalry, evidently moving at walking pace to begin with, but gradually gathering speed. The impression of urgency is emphasized as the riders lower their lances – the caption simply notes that they 'came to fight against King Harold'.

The initial advance is slowed down as William, carrying a commander's baton, interrogates Vital about the whereabouts of the English. The caption states, 'Here Duke William asks Vital if he has seen Harold's army.' Vital is pointing behind him, where two knights are taking up position on some rising ground which is unusually depicted as a hillock. It could also be interpreted as open ground, as towards the bottom of this hill on the right-hand side there are three trees, perhaps indicating forest. More likely they represent just more visual punctuation, because on the other side is a mirror image of the Vital scene, where an armed soldier on foot is telling 'Harold about William's army' and he too is pointing behind him. Harold is shown mounted for the only time during the battle. There is another soldier in this scene, who is peering back into the trees. Both soldiers are standing on what appears to be unusually uneven ground, the significance of which is unclear.

Another stylized tree marks the beginning of the next phase of the battle. William, still carrying his baton, is delivering a speech to his troops – 'Duke William tells his soldiers to prepare themselves manfully and wisely for the battle against the army of the English.'

One of the knights is turning his head to listen to the duke, while the other cavalrymen are commencing a rapid advance towards the English lines. From this

Bayeux Tapestry. William addresses troops telling them to prepare themselves manfully and wisely for battle against the English army.

point the pace quickens, as the Norman vanguard moves towards the English under covering fire from the archers. Almost all the knights are holding their lances like javelins; they may have been preparing to throw them, but this was the standard way of holding such weapons in the eleventh century. Towards the end of this scene the horses are shown at full gallop, with all hooves off the ground. They are also shown to be running in a group for the first time, rather than in single file; this gives the impression of breadth to the attack. At the front of the cavalry charge, the first Norman casualties, brought down by English spears, are seen under the horses' hooves. From now onwards, the casualties from both sides fill the lower border of the Tapestry.

At this point, the Normans meet the English shield wall, which is here shown facing in both directions to meet the Normans. The two armies are shown fighting on the same level surface; no attempt is made here to depict the hill on which the English army made its stand.

Without interruption, but with a change of direction, the next scene portrays the deaths of Harold's two brothers Leofwine and Gyrth. Apart from Harold, they are the only named casualties shown on the Tapestry. They appear to have been cut down by the lances of the Norman cavalry, although in reality it is not known how or precisely when they died. Their deaths were particularly important to the English because they were directly in line to the throne and their deaths removed the immediate successors to Harold from the scene.

Bayeux Tapestry. The armies engage with Norman cavalry attacking the English shield wall. The wall would have been up to ten men deep, with the elite housecarls at the front and ordinary troops of the *fyrd* behind.

The Malfosse (see bottom picture, p. 182)

The caption of the next scene simply states, 'Here English and French fell together in the fight' and the two sides are shown butchering each other with swords and battleaxes at the height of the battle. This leads into an episode where the local topography played a major role. It shows horses and riders falling dramatically into an area of water with pointed stakes, or possibly reeds, protruding upwards. This may have been one of the natural marshy hollows that are found around Battle. It could have been a deliberate trap built by the English for the Normans, although there are no contemporary references to such a device. The Tapestry here seems to be recording the episode of the Malfosse, where a large number of Normans were brought down by a marshy ditch.

The chroniclers all report that the onslaught of William's cavalry was brought to a halt at one stage by a ditch in which knights and horses came to grief. The *Battle*

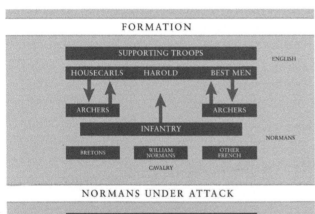

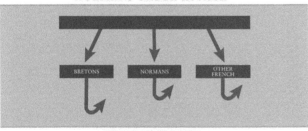

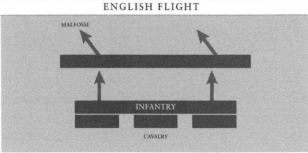

A conventional plan of the Battle of Hastings.

Abbey Chronicle, written in the mid-twelfth century, calls the ditch the 'Malfosse'. The chronicler Wace does not name the ditch, but emphasizes the heavy casualties the Normans took there. However, there is no agreement about when this incident occurred. Wace places it within the main assault, as does the Tapestry, but William of Jumièges and the *Battle Abbey Chronicle* report that it occurred after Harold's death, when the Norman troops were chasing the vanquished English off the battlefield. If the disaster was part of the final rout, then the ditch in question could be a partly filled natural gulley running about a kilometre beyond the abbey church. This gulley appears as 'Manfosse' in a 1279 document.[4] If it took place during the main assault, then the ditch would have been at the foot of the hill at the top of which the English held their ground. If we accept the conventional interpretation of where the battle was fought, this is an area known as the Asten Valley. The caption at this point simply reports, 'Here English and French fell together in the fight.'

The Malfosse scene leads directly on to the depiction of a hill, on which the English are facing attack from both directions – which once again is using poetic licence. The hill is depicted in the form of a wavy line leading to a flat summit,

Bayeux Tapestry. The representation of a hill in this scene, on which the English are being harassed by the Norman cavalry, is the most specific attempt by the Tapestry to illustrate the topography of the battlefield. It is possible that the scene captures events after the feigned retreat, when the English lines broke and were penetrated by the enemy. It is equally possible that the English are depicted as facing in both directions as a device to increase the drama of events.

reaching just over halfway up in the main register. Taken literally, it represents a steep-sided, high hill, with a very narrow plateau at the top which can only just accommodate four English soldiers. Therefore, it in no way gives an accurate picture of the geography of the battlefield, although it does emphasize the relative locations of the two armies. Curiously, none of the defending English soldiers are shown wearing chain mail, and two of them, who are falling headlong off the hill, are apparently unarmed. The hill scene marks the only attempt to realistically represent the lie of the land on which the battle was fought.

The Tapestry does not appear to depict one of the best known incidents in the story of the battle – the feigned retreat. Towards the end of the day, having attacked the English shield wall again, the Norman cavalry retreated, but instead of regrouping at the foot of the hill they continued to ride away as if leaving the battlefield. Thinking that they had won the day, one arm of the shield wall broke away and pursued the Normans down the hill, only to be turned on and cut down by the returning Norman knights.

Bayeux Tapestry. Bishop Odo depicted here holding a baton, at the height of battle encouraging the Norman troops, who may have been losing heart at this stage.

Baudri of Bourgueil recounts the story of the retreat and it is repeated by the English chronicler Henry of Huntingdon (*c*.1088–*c*.1157). William of Poitiers writes, 'The Normans and their allies, realizing that they could not overcome an enemy so numerous and standing so firm without loss to themselves, retreated, deliberately feigning flight.' According to Poitiers, this tactic was repeated twice. Some historians doubt if it happened at all and if an eleventh-century cavalry force would have had the necessary discipline to attempt such a manoeuvre without itself losing formation and being scattered. There is, however, evidence of the tactic having been used elsewhere by the Normans: at Saint-Aubin-le-Cauf near Arques in 1052–53 and near Messina in Sicily in 1060.[5]

The next episode in the Tapestry is actually concerned with flight and is linked to a rumour that Duke William has been killed or seriously wounded. Some of the Normans begin to panic, but Odo is there to calm them down. (See p. 179).

The bishop urges the flagging soldiers to return to the fight and then goes back to the thick of battle where he makes the reluctant cavalrymen turn, stop and attack. Wace reported that Odo addressed these young noblemen, whose task it was to guard equipment, by saying, 'Stand still, stand still! Calm down and do not move! Do not fear anything, for, please God, we will win the day.' Wace continued:

> Odo went back to where the battle was at its fiercest; that day he had truly shown his worth … he sat on an all white horse and everyone recognized him. He held a club in his hand, made the knights head for where the need was greatest and brought them to a stop there. He often made them attack and often made them strike.[6]

Although Wace was writing much later than Hastings, he was a canon of Bayeux and would have been familiar with the Tapestry and with the other principal sources. Therefore, his account cannot be totally discounted and perhaps the best way to describe Odo's role at Hastings is 'support and command'. The rumour, of course, is false and in the next scene William raises his visor to show his face and the troops are reassured. 'Here is Duke William' the caption affirms.

Odo's central role in the English campaign depicted on the Tapestry is not repeated by contemporary accounts. Most descriptions of Odo at Hastings rely on the story told in the Tapestry, which is just as Odo would have wanted it to be. There is little documentary evidence to suggest that Odo played a fighting role at the Battle of Hastings. William of Poitiers, writing much closer to the events of 1066, mentions the presence of the two bishops, Odo and Geoffrey of Coutances, together with numerous clergy and a few monks, and that the assembly prepared for combat by prayer. He also states that Odo never took arms and never wished to. The *Song of Hastings* and Orderic Vitalis do not mention Odo at Hastings.

The bishop is shown carrying a mace-like implement, which has been variously interpreted as a club or a commander's baton. No other contemporary source gives Odo such a prominent place in the proceedings and none records him actually participating in the fighting. As a priest, it was forbidden for him to spill blood, but the Tapestry shows Odo in the midst of the battle and, significantly, a later papal enquiry into the slaughter at Hastings required the Norman clerics to give penance for shedding blood in the battle. William of Poitiers virtually implies that Odo joined the fighting when he explains that the bishop 'helped in war by his most practical counsels as far as his religion allowed ... and was most singularly and steadfastly loyal to [William], whom he cherished with so great a love that he would not be willingly separated from him even on the battlefield'. In the battle scene on the Tapestry, Odo is wearing a gambeson – a padded jacket – over his hauberk, which is short compared to the longer version worn by the fighting soldiers. It is argued, therefore, that as he was dressed defensively, he was a non-combatant.[7] It is true that Wace records that, 'The Bishop of Bayeux ... conducted himself very nobly' when hearing confessions and giving blessings before the Battle of Hastings. The Norman chroniclers contrast the behaviour of the two armies on the night before the battle. The Norman soldiers piously prayed and made confession, while the English army drank and sang. The Tapestry does not depict either of these activities; the nearest it gets is in the portrayal of Odo blessing the meal in the pre-battle banqueting scene.

The Death of King Harold

The border beneath the last scene shows a long line of archers advancing with their bows ready to fire, perhaps emphasizing the role that they played in the final victory. The archers are supporting the Norman cavalry, who now return to the charge in good order for one final onslaught on the English housecarls surrounding the king. The caption reports that, 'Here the French fight and those who were with Harold fell.' The action unfolds amidst considerable confusion. The Normans are seen attacking the English from both sides, but this time it is a more accurate representation of what was actually happening towards the end of the battle. Having pierced the English lines, the Normans could surround the surviving troops who were protecting Harold.

These final scenes portray both the chaos and the brutality that characterized the demise of Harold and the English army. Scenes of dismembered bodies and the looting of the dead illustrate the lower frieze, while in the main narrative an unarmed English prisoner is about to be executed. The most striking figure in this scene is a knight riding to the left on a finely harnessed stallion; his black shield is decorated with a dragon. The Tapestry gives no clue as to the identification of the rider.

The penultimate caption simply states, 'Here King Harold is slain' but the interpretation of the manner of his death is far from simple and has been subject

Bayeux Tapestry. The English shield wall is here portrayed as facing in two directions. The only English archer in the battle depicted on the Tapestry is seen here in the centre of the picture.

to much debate and controversy. The warrior standing directly beneath the name 'Harold' is the most likely candidate.

The king appears to have been struck in the eye with an arrow, which he is apparently trying to pull out. Alternatively, the figure of a knight slumped over his horse's neck under 'Rex' could be the king, or it might be the axe-wielding soldier to the right who has been brought down by a blow to the thigh. At least three of the

Bayeux Tapestry. One of the most graphic scenes on the Tapestry shows horses and riders falling at the foot of the hill. They seem to have been tripped by an obstacle, in the form of wooden stakes projecting from water. This could represent the event called the Malfosse, where a large number of Normans died. The chroniclers describe the Malfosse as a natural depression, but here the Tapestry could be implying that it was a man-made trap.

Bayeux Tapestry. The caption simply observes 'Here King Harold is killed'. It has been commonly assumed that the king was slain by an arrow in his eye, although the depiction of the arrow is a modern restoration. However, it does appear that the restored needlework is broadly authentic; the needle holes indicate that it closely replicates the original. Several of the chroniclers also argue that an arrow in the eye was the cause of the Harold's death.

chronicles agree that an arrow to the eye was the cause of Harold's death, but the same tradition adds that after he had been wounded, he was struck on the thigh by a sword. The Tapestry may have been trying to portray both of these events. Irrespective of the cause, the king was dead, the English were defeated and the battle was over.

There are fewer disputes about the location of his death, although even on this issue we cannot be absolutely certain. William founded an abbey on the site of the battle, with the high altar of the church located on the spot where Harold died. The *Battle Abbey Chronicle* specifies that this is where the defeated king's standard was toppled. William of Malmesbury (*c.*1095–*c.*1143) also records that the high altar stood where Harold's corpse was found, surrounded by a heap of bodies.

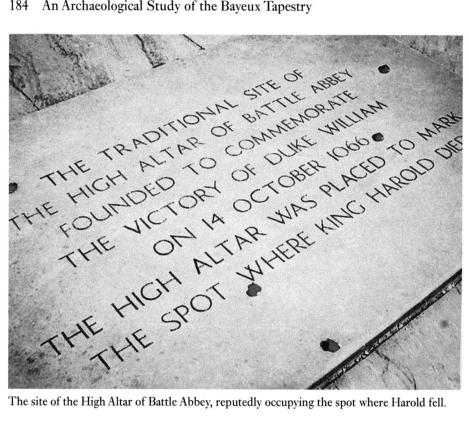

The site of the High Altar of Battle Abbey, reputedly occupying the spot where Harold fell.

The Benedictine abbey at Battle was started about 1070, partly as a penance for the bloodshed at the battle, but also as a colonial statement of Norman supremacy. The construction of the abbey was part of an arrangement made between the pope and King William in about 1070, when William was recognized by papal legates but simultaneously suffered the heavy penalties imposed for the excessive bloodshed involved in the conquest of England.

Although the eastern arm of Battle Abbey church was sufficiently complete to allow for its consecration in 1076, it was not until 1094 that the finished church was finally consecrated in the presence of William II, the Archbishop of Canterbury and seven bishops. On his death, the Conqueror bequeathed to the community at Battle his royal cloak, a collection of relics and a portable altar used during his military campaigns. He had also endowed the abbey with extensive estates, including all the land within a radius of a mile and a half (2.5km) of the high altar.

Within this specified area around the abbey, the abbot enjoyed a unique jurisdiction over land and men. William's gift promoted Battle to the rank of fifteenth wealthiest religious house in England. The abbey was dissolved by Henry VIII in 1538 and much of its fabric, including the church, was destroyed. The site was partially cleared and in 1903 a memorial marking the location of Harold's death was placed on the site of the high altar. The site lies on a narrow ridge

Battle Abbey seen from the valley to the south-west, possibly marking the site of the Malfosse.

on open heathland and in order to build the abbey it was necessary to undertake extensive terracing and the construction of a massive undercroft.

Those English troops who survived sought cover in the country to the north at dusk. Some of them turned in acts of final defiance to inflict further losses on their Norman enemies. Baudri describes in lengthy and gory detail how the blood-roused Normans pursue and slaughter the hapless English, so that future war will be avoided. Only nightfall mercifully puts an end to the carnage and allows the vanquished to crawl away into hiding or to die. At daybreak, William pressed his fighters forward with another speech, in which he indicates they had best strike while the English were still disorganized and the cities and towns vulnerable. It was their only chance for a quick victory and the establishment of peace.

Air view of Battle Abbey. The remains of the abbey now houses a school. In the background is St Mary's, the parish church of Battle.

Norman chroniclers noted with pride that some of the most famous Norman fighters of their day died at Hastings, but it was the English who had lost their king and most of their nobility. One authority has described the battle as a 'conflict between the military methods of the seventh century and those of the eleventh century'. It was the major and final act in the death of the Anglo-Scandinavian military tradition of the shield wall.

The last scene of the Tapestry shows a group of cavalrymen, swords aloft, pursuing the defeated English. The horsemen are largely portrayed in the conventional manner of the Tapestry and appear to be authentic, although there are anomalies, such as the rider who appears to be astride two horses – or no horse at all! There is also a stunted tree which does not conform to the design of the other trees on the Tapestry. Finally at the very end, the Tapestry is torn and fragmented; on these remnants there is a group of eight badly depicted English troops, who are divided by a green wavy line. Above the line there are four men on foot, one of whom appears to have an arrow in his eye is following an unarmed horseman. Below the line are two curiously dressed horsemen and what appears to be a jester – all are spurious later additions.

The *Carmen* reported that:

> The corpses of the English, strewn upon the ground, he [William] left to be devoured by worms and wolves, by birds and dogs. Harold's dismembered body he gathered together, and wrapped what he had gathered in fine purple linen; and returning to his camp by the sea, he bore it with him, that he might carry out the customary funeral rites.

After the Battle

After the battle, William expected that the surviving English aristocracy would submit to him. When no word was received from the English leaders after five days, he marched north-east along the coast, attacking and garrisoning ports on the way in order to secure his communications across the Channel. After taking Dover, where he was joined by Norman reinforcements from France, he marched inland to the metropolitan city of Canterbury. As they went, the Norman forces plundered the land, destroying villages and farms. No direct account of the havoc the Normans caused has survived, but Domesday Book (1086) records numerous manors in southern England whose value had been reduced, presumably as a result of the passage of William's armies and their raiding parties. William and his army appear to have been delayed on their progress northwards by an outbreak of dysentery at Dover, but after they recovered they proceeded to Southwark on the River Thames to the south of London Bridge. Here, a curious incident took place in the form of a skirmish between the Normans and Londoners led by Edgar the Atheling, now the uncrowned king of England. The Normans boasted that here 'they dealt a double blow on the pride of [William's] stubborn foes' and gave Edgar 'a bloody nose', but they did not cross the bridge. Clearly, William did not feel capable of taking London at that stage and, having set fire to Southwark, he moved westwards up the Thames Valley in an effort to isolate the capital. As he travelled, he began to receive submissions from the Anglo-Saxons, now convinced that the duke would become the next English king. Edward the Confessor's widow, Edith, conceded Winchester and the treasury of England at an early stage, while Archbishop Stigand travelled to Wallingford from London to swear his allegiance to William. Here William crossed the Thames and built a castle before turning east along the ancient trackway called the Icknield Way at the foot of the Chilterns. Eventually, the Normans encamped at Berkhamsted to await the surrender of London.

Isolated, defenceless and threatened with famine by the systematic devastation that accompanied William's circuitous march, London surrendered. While at

Berkhamsted, William was met by 'Archbishop Aldred and the Atheling, Edgar and Earl Edwin and Earl Morcar, and all the chief men of London. And they submitted after most damage had been done … and they gave hostages, and he promised that he would be a gracious liege lord.' Eventually, on Christmas Day 1066, William's coronation took place in Westminster Abbey, accompanied by riots in the streets of London; the 'year of the four kings' came to an end with the ultimate Norman triumph.

The Missing End Section

For much of its life, the Tapestry was kept in the cathedral at Bayeux. It was displayed for a fortnight once a year; the rest of the time it was folded in a cedar chest in the church. Undoubtedly, this restricted exposure was a factor in its remarkable preservation. The last portion of the Tapestry, which would have been at the top of the chest, would have been handled most and was most subject to decay. Accordingly, about 2.5–3m (8–10ft) of the final section is missing.

There has been much speculation about the contents of the lost section of the Bayeux Tapestry. After the battle, William made his way along the south-east coast of England to Dover, destroying towns such as Rye on the way. He then travelled to London through Canterbury and Rochester. There was a skirmish on London Bridge, but the duke did not enter the capital at this point. Instead, he took his army along the Thames Valley as far as Wallingford, where he crossed the River Thames and then turned back along the foot of the Chiltern Hills. At Berkhamsted he negotiated the surrender of London and was then crowned King of England on Christmas Day 1066.

The missing piece of the Tapestry could not have captured all of that in the limited space available as it would have only had room for three or four scenes, the last of which would almost certainly have been the coronation of the new king. It might have included the surrender of Canterbury, the headquarters of the English Church, and possibly the river crossing at Wallingford and the negotiations at Berkhamsted. It is most unlikely that the contents of the missing section will ever be known, but a brave effort has recently been made to resolve the mystery. A reconstruction of the final part of the Tapestry was created by a community project on the island of Alderney in the Channel Islands in 2012–13.[8] The first of the new scenes shows William at a victory feast with his half-brothers, Odo and Robert, in front of a tent surrounded by the corpses of English soldiers. The next scene shows the nobles of London surrendering to William and his knights at Berkhamsted. Finally, in a scene reminiscent of Harold's coronation at the beginning of 1066, William is being crowned by Aeldred, the Archbishop of York, and Geoffrey, Bishop of Coutances. Outside Westminster Abbey church the new king is being acclaimed by the English, while finishing touches are being given to the newly built Tower of London.

Bayeux Tapestry. The end of the surviving Tapestry, which shows the defeated English troops leaving the battlefield, is largely the result of poor nineteenth century restoration.

The Alderney Tapestry, completed in 2013, provides a version of the missing end of the Bayeux Tapestry envisaging that it showed William the Conqueror's coronation on Christmas Day 1066. The caption reads: 'Here Duke William ate. Here the nobles of London gathered. Here William was given the royal crown. And here the Englishmen proclaimed the king'. The tapestry's permanent home is in the Alderney Library. To mark the 950th anniversary of the Battle of Hastings, in 2016 the Alderney Tapestry was exhibited at different historical locations in the UK and Channel Islands.

Conclusion

For long the popular perception of the Norman Conquest of England has been based on the graphic images found on the Bayeux Tapestry. In particular, the battle scenes have coloured the way in which generations have viewed the defeat of King Harold and the English army at Hastings. Increasingly, however, the historical accuracy of the events depicted on the Tapestry has been brought into question and today it is viewed as a partial and particular version of the Norman Conquest. As narrative history the Tapestry now stands alongside the accounts of the contemporary chroniclers like William of Poitiers or William of Jumièges; that is, to be treated as an invaluable reservoir of information, but not necessarily to be taken literally. This more critical approach has been extended to the specific material images on the Tapestry. No longer is it possible to take the Tapestry's version of, for instance, dress or architecture at face value as representing an authentic picture of life in the mid eleventh century. Just as the Tapestry's account of the events of 1066 is impressionistic, so is its geography and depiction of the physical world.

Much recent research into the Bayeux Tapestry has concentrated on identifying the sources for the images found on the hanging. Lewis and Owen-Crocker amongst others have emphasized the importance of late Saxon manuscripts as a source for much of the Tapestry's iconography.[9] Despite the extensive existing literature on the Tapestry, there is now room for a new definitive analysis of the sources for the images which would bring together the results of all research into the topic.

The lack of historical and topographic authenticity should not lead to any reduction in the assessment of the value of the Tapestry as a unique historical document. The recent reassessment of the Tapestry's contents has served to emphasize the complexity and skilful design of the hanging. The Bayeux Tapestry is a tightly structured work with intricate cross-referencing and balancing of individual images and scenes throughout its length. The designer was economical with detail, but everything that is included is deliberate with a purpose, even if that purpose is not immediately obvious.

We cannot use the Tapestry as a handbook to the archaeology or landscape of the Normans, but virtually every scene provides pointers to the real world it was representing; added to which, the Tapestry creates its own landscape through the subtle juxtaposition of images. We may not be presented with realistic versions of Bosham, Ponthieu, the Breton Marches, Bayeux, Westminster, Pevensey or the battlefield in the eleventh century, but we are given acceptable impressions of these places and landscapes and on occasion we do seem to be looking at a genuine landscape. For example, in the boatbuilding scenes, although the pictures showing the progression from growing trees to completed vessels retain a cartoon element, there is a sense of authenticity in the details of the work of the woodmen and carpenters. Similarly, in the scenes around Mont-St-Michel it is possible to believe in the Norman soldiers sinking into the estuarine mudflats of the River Cousenon. The depiction of Edward the Confessor's funeral cortège provides us with a unique and credible version of that event. The section of the Tapestry devoted to the Battle of Hastings is presented with little indication of the landscape in which the conflict took place. The appearance of a hill, on which the English are fighting, contrasts to the close-up cavalry and infantry combat which characterizes most of the battle section. This hint at the topography of the battlefield shrewdly reveals its landscape, through the mist created by the images of intense individual hostilities. In this, as in so many other areas, the Tapestry is unique. There are few who would argue with the current conservator of the Tapestry, Sylvette Lemagnen, who observed that the hanging 'is one of the supreme achievements of the Norman Romanesque ... . Its survival almost intact over nine centuries is little short of miraculous ... . Its exceptional length, the harmony and freshness of its colours, its exquisite workmanship, and the genius of its guiding spirit combine to make it endlessly fascinating.'[10]

Notes

Introduction
1. Stenton, 1965, 23.
2. Pastan *et al* 2014.
3. Pastan *et al* 2014.
4. Hicks 2006, 32.
5. Grape 1994, 28–9.
6. Brown 1998, 41–2.
7. Maclagan 1943, 24.
8. Archer 1894, 1–4.
9. Wilson 1985.
10. Brooks *et al* 1978, 1–34.
11. Lewis 2005; Lewis 2008; Hyer *et al* 2015.
12. Foys *et al* 2009; Lewis *et al* 2011; Pastan *et al* 2014.
13. Davis *et al* 1998; van Houts 1995; Chibnall 1968–80.

Chapter 1
1. Dodwell 1966, 49.
2. Caple 2006, 80.
3. Hayward 1998, 90.
4. Musset 2002, 23–5.
5. Brown *et al* 1994, 55–74.
6. Beech 2011.
7. Stenton 1965, 9..
8. Woodman 2015, 68.
9. Hicks 2006, 29–39.
10. Pastan *et al* 2014, 7.
11. Owen-Crocker 1986, 134.
12. Caple 2006, 84.
13. Clegg Hyer 2012, 60.
14. Hill and McSween 2011, 44–51.
15. Lewis 2005, 143.
16. See image 10 and 11.
17. Owen-Crocker 2009, 51–96.
18. Hart 1999, 115–67.
19. Hart 1999, 161.
20. Howe 2008, 16.
21. Howe 2008, 39.

22. Hoskins 1955, 46.
23. Karkov 2010, 157–68.
24. Hill 2010, 169–74.
25. Bloch 2006, 75–8.
26. Lewis 2005, 21.
27. Hart 1999, 117–68.
28. Pastan *et al* 2014, 208.
29. Schwartz 1994.
30. Chadwick 1922.

Chapter 2

1. Oksanen 2012, 158.
2. Gardiner 1999, 78.
3. Biddle 1985, 51–72.
4. Grape 1994.
5. Thomas *et al* 2012.
6. James 1997, 39–40.
7. Russo 1998, 113.
8. Biddle 1976, 296.
9. Biddle 1987, 315.
10. Biddle 1976, 299.
11. Lethaby 1906.
12. Henig 2015, 23–33.
13. Schofield 1993, 30.
14. Sullivan 1994, 57.
15. Thomas 2002, 16–17.
16. Thomas *et al* 2006, 44–6.
17. Thomas 2002, 16–18.
18. Steane 2003, 72.
19. Mason 1996, 17.
20. Thomas *et al* 2006.
21. Neagley 2011.
22. Hart 1999, 155. The Eadwine Psalter was adapted form an earlier Carolingian Psalter.
23. Marvin 2006, 27–8.
24. Thomas 2010.
25. Oggins 2004, 39–40.
26. Williams 2008, 123.
27. Williams 2008, 123.
28. Gautier 2007, 52–3.
29. Williams 2008, 124–7.
30. Hutchinson 1994, 171.
31. Salzman 1953, 183.
32. Blair 2006, 329.
33. Kirby 1978, 164.

34. Gem 1985, 32–6.
35. Musset 2005, 94.
36. Woodman 2015.
37. Lewis 2008, 103–4.
38. Hart 1999, 134.
39. Heslop 2003, 276.
40. Salzman 1953, 182.
41. Goodburn 1993.
42. Stalley 1999, 88–9.
43. MacDougal 2009.
44. Pastan *et al* 2014, 196, 135.

Chapter 3
 1. McGrail 1983, 144–8.
 2. Lewis 2005, 71.
 3. Lewis 2008, 132.
 4. Hill 1990, 51–8.
 5. Taylor 1992.
 6. Gauthiez 2013, 21–3.
 7. Bates 1993.
 8. Gauthiez 2013, 23.
 9. Le Maho 2000.
10. Le Maho 2000, 73–5.
11. Chibnall 1969–80, iv, 290.
12. Impey 2002.
13. Dodd 2003.
14. Stephenson 2011, 71–4.
15. Beech 2011, 10–16, but see also Lewis 2007, 100–20.
16. Lewis 2005, 22.
17. Pastan *et al* 2014, 194.
18. www.ot-montsaintmichel.com.

Chapter 4
 1. Pastan et al 2014, 120.
 2. Pounds 1994, 12.
 3. Allen Brown 2004, 16.
 4. Jones 1988, 20.
 5. Allen Brown 2004, 15.
 6. Allen Brown 2004, 41.
 7. Armitage 1912, 147–8.
 8. Higham *et al* 1992, 97.
 9. Sanquer 1977.
10. Meirion-Jones *et al* 1993, 165.
11. Jones 1988, 21.
12. Musset 2005, 67.

13. Woodman 2015, 63.
14. Jones 1988.
15. Higham *et al* 1992.
16. Morillo 1994, 141.
17. Higham *et al* 1982.
18. Jones 1988, 22.
19. Hosler 2007.
20. Higham *et al* 1992, 99.
21. La Borderie 1899, 18.
22. Hayward Gallery 1984, 154–5.
23. Jones 1988, 17.
24. M. Kneen, pers. comm.
25. Allen Brown 2004, 9.
26. Griffiths 1981, 520–1.
27. Musset 2002, 214.
28. Owen-Crocker 2009.
29. Higham *et al* 1992, 154.
30. Barker *et al* 2000.
31. Gameson 1997.

Chapter 5

 1. Brown 2009.
 2. Bartlett 2013, 315.
 3. Davis *et al* 1998, 124–5.
 4. Chibnall 1969–80, ii, 172–3.
 5. Crook 2011, 115.
 6. Bernstein 1982, 53.
 7. Foys 2009, 158–75.
 8. Bentley 1985, 37.
 9. Calkins 1980, 116.
10. Burgess 2004, 154–5.
11. www.learn.columbia.edu.
12. Wilson 1985, 180.
13. Musset 2002, 152.
14. Foys *et al* 2009, 36–7.
15. Davis *et al* 1998, 71.
16. Hart 1999.
17. Sherlock *et al* 1988, 1121.
18. Gem 1997, 90–122.
19. Overbey 2009, 36. Presumably the Roi element of the place name was added after William became king of England.
20. www.mondes-normands.caen.fr.
21. Pastan *et al* 2014, 113.
22. Neveux 1996.
23. Allen 2009, 135.

24. Allen 2009, 128.
25. Bates 2004–16.
26. Renoux 1995, 195–6.
27. Bates 1975.
28. Herrick 2007, 39.
29. de Nogent 1910, 15–22.
30. Foys *et al* 2009, 42.
31. Pastan *et al* 2014, 68.
32. Rowley 2013.
33. Pastan *et al* 2014, 265.
34. Musset 2002, 156.
.35. www.culture24.org.uk.

Chapter 6
 1. Thomson *et al* 1999, 214.
 2. Rodwell *et al* 2015, 52–3.
 3. Steane 1993, 165.
 4. Rodwell 2015.
 5. Lewis 107.
 6. Woodman 2015.
 7. Barlow, *Vita* 113.
 8. Musset 2002, 162.
 9. Williams 2004–16.
10. Higham 1997, 174.
11. Musset 2002, 168.
12. Church 2006, 19–29.
13. Church 2006, 30.
14. Higham 1997, 175.
15. Keats-Rohan 2012.
16. Brown 1988, 167–77.
17. Brown *et al* 1994, 144.

Chapter 7
 1. Burgess 2004.
 2. van Houts 1988, 159–183.
 3. Gillmor 1996, 114–128.
 4 . Davis 1987, 74.
 5. Brown *et al* 1994, 55–73.
 6. Olsen *et al* 1967, 74–153.
 7. McGrail 1988, 150.
 8. Lewis 2005, 68 n. 427.
 9. Hutchinson 1994, 8.
10. Lewis 2005, n. 437.
11. McGrail 1988, 160.
12. Musset 2002, 190.

13. de Smet 1981, 301–309.
14. Lebecq 2011.
15. Bachrach 1985.
16. Morillo 1994, 124–8.
17. Musset 2002, 190.
18. Clark 2004, 25.
19. Davis 1987. Chapter 8

Chapter 8
1. van Houts 1997.
2. McGrail 1983, 255.
3. Cole 2013.
4. Baker *et al* 2013, 353.
5. Combes *et al* 1995.
6. Hooke 1998,142–4.
7. See image 85.
8. Austin 2010.
9. Wessex Archaeology 1996.
10. Rowley 1999, 75.
11. Pastan *et al* 2014, 134–7.

Chapter 9
1. Austin 2010.
2. www.channel4.com.
3. Musset 2002, 218.
4. Stevenson 1913, 292–303.
5. Allen Brown 1996, 212–13.
6. Burgess 2004, 8121–8.
7. Legge 1987, 84–5.
8. www.alderneybayeuxtapestry.com
9. Lewis 2005; Lewis 2008; Owen-Crocker 2015.
10. Lemagnen 2015.

Bibliography

Allen Brown, R.A. (2004) English *Castles*. Woodbridge: Boydell & Brewer.

Allen Brown, R.A. (1996) The Battle of Hastings. In S. Morillo (ed.), *The Battle of Hastings*. Woodbridge: Boydell & Brewer.

Allen, R. (2009) 'The Norman Episcopate, 989–1110;, PhD thesis, 2 vols, University of Glasgow.

Austin, N. (2010) *The Secrets of the Norman Invasion*. Crowhurst: Ogmium Press.

Baker, J. and S. Brookes (2013) *Beyond the Burghal Hidage*. Leiden: Brill.

Bartlett, R. (2013) *Why Can the Dead Do Such Great Things? Saints and Worshippers from the Martyrs to the Reformation*. Princeton: Princeton University Press.

Bates, D. (2004–11) Odo, earl of Kent (d.1097), bishop of Bayeux and magnate. In *Oxford Dictionary of National Biography*. Oxford: Oxford University Press.

Bates, D. (1993) Rouen. In Stratford, J., *Medieval Art, Architecture and Archaeology at Rouen*. The British Archaeological Association, XII.

Bates, D. (1975) The character and career of Odo, Bishop of Bayeux (1049/50-1097). *Speculum* 1, Jan 1975.

Baudwin, P., (2004) *La Premiere Normandie (xe–xle siècles)*. Caen: Presses universitaires de Caen.

Beech, G.T. (2011) The Breton Campaign and the possibility that the Bayeux Tapestry was produced in the Loire Valley (St Florent of Saumur). In M.J. Lewis, G.R. Owen-Crocker, and D. Terkla (eds.), *The Bayeux Tapestry: New Approaches*. Oxford: Oxbow Books.

Bentley, J. (1985) *Restless Bones: The Story of Relics*. London: Constable.

Bernstein, D. (1982) The blinding of Harold. In *Anglo-Norman Studies* V. Woodbridge: Boydell & Brewer.

Biddle, M. (1976) *Winchester Studies 1: Winchester in the Middle Ages*. Oxford: Clarendon Press.

Biddle M. (1985) Seasonal festivals and residence: Winchester, Westminster and Gloucester in the tenth to twelfth centuries. In *Anglo-Norman Studies* VIII. Woodbridge: Boydell & Brewer.

Biddle, M. (1987) Early Norman Winchester. In J.C. Holt (ed.), *Domesday Studies*. Woodbridge: Boydell & Brewer.

Blair, J. (2006) *The Church in Anglo-Saxon Society*. Oxford: Oxford University Press.

Bloch, R.H. (2006) *A Needle in the Right Hand of God: The Norman Conquest of 1066 and the Making and Meaning of the Bayeux Tapestry*. London: Random House.

Bouet, P. and Desbordes, O. eds. (2005), *Cartulaire du Mont-St-Michel*, Les amis du Mont-St Michel.

Brown, S.A. (1988) *The Bayeux Tapestry: History and Bibliography*. Woodbridge: Boydell Press.

Brown, S.A. (2009) Auctoritas, Consilium et Auxilium: Images of Authority in the Bayeux Tapestry. In M.K. Foys, K.E. Overbey and D. Terkla (eds.), *The Bayeux Tapestry: New Interpretations*. Woodbridge: Boydell & Brewer.

Brown, S.A. and M.W. Herren (1994) The Adelae Comitissae of Baudri de Bourgueil and the Bayeux Tapestry. In *Anglo-Norman Studies* 16. Woodbridge: Boydell & Brewer.

Burgess, G.S. (tr.) (2004) *The History of the Norman People: Wace's Roman de Rou*. Woodbridge: Boydell & Brewer.

Calkins, R.G. (1980) *Monuments of Medieval Art*. Ithaca, New York: Cornell University Press.

Caple, C. (2006) *Objects: Reluctant Witnesses to the Past*. London: Routledge.

Carson, R.A.G. (2013) *Mints, Dies and Currency*. London: Routledge.

Chibnall, M. (ed. and tr.) (1968-80) *The Ecclesiastical History of Orderic Vitalis* 6 vols. Oxford: Clarendon Press.

Church, S.D. (2006) The death of the king. In *Anglo-Norman Studies* 29. Woodbridge: Boydell and Brewer.

Clark, J. (ed.) (2004) *The Medieval Horse and its Equipment, c.1150–c.1450*. Woodbridge: Boydell Press.

Clegg Hyer, M. (2012) Reduce, reuse, recycle: Imagined and reimagined textiles in Anglo-Saxon England. In R. Netherton and G.R. Owen-Crocker (eds.), *Medieval Clothing and Textiles* 8, Woodbridge: Boydell & Brewer.

Cole, A. (2013) The place name evidence for a routeway network in early medieval England. *BAR British Series* 589.

Combes, P. and M. Lyne (1995) Hastings, Hastingaceaster and Haestingaport: a question of identity. *Sussex Archaeological Collection* vol.133.

Crook, J. (2011) *English Medieval Shrines*. Woodbridge: Boydell & Brewer.

Davis, R.C.H. (1987) The warhorses of the Normans. In *Anglo-Norman Studies* X. Woodbridge: Boydell & Brewer.

Davis, R.C.H. and M. Chibnall (eds. and tr.) (1998) *The Gesta Guillelmi of William of Poitiers*. Oxford: Clarendon Press.

de Nogent, Guibert (1910) A treatise on relics. In C.G. Coulton (ed. and tr.), *Life in the Middle Ages*. vol I. New York: Macmillan.

Dodwell, C.R. (1966) The Bayeux Tapestry and the French secular epic. *The Burlington Magazine* 108, no. 764, Nov 1966.

Foys, M.K. (2009) Pulling the Arrow Out: The Legend of Harold's Death and the Bayeux Tapestry. In M.K. Foys, K.E. Overbey and D. Terkla (eds.), *The Bayeux Tapestry: New Interpretations*. Woodbridge: The Boydell Press.

Gameson, R. (1997) *The Study of the Bayeux Tapestry*, Woodbridge: Boydell and Brewer.

Gardiner M. (1999) Shipping and trade between England and the Continent during the eleventh century. In *Anglo-Norman Studies* XXII. Woodbridge: Boydell & Brewer.

Gauthiez, B. (2013) The urban development of Rouen, 989–1345. In L.V. Hicks and E. Brenner (eds.), *Society and Culture in Medieval Rouen*. Turnhout, Belgium: Brepols Publishers.

Gautier, A. (2007) Game parks in Sussex. In *Anglo-Norman Studies* 29. Woodbridge: Boydell & Brewer.

Gem, R. (1985) Holy Trinity Church, Bosham. *Archaeological Journal* 142.

Gem, R. (1980) The Romanesque rebuilding of Westminster Abbey. In *Anglo-Norman Studies* 3. Woodbridge: Boydell & Brewer.

Gillmor, C.M. (1996) Naval logistics of the cross-Channel operation 1066. In S. Morillo, *The Battle of Hastings: Sources and Interpretations*. Woodbridge: Boydell & Brewer.

Goodburn, D. (1995) Fragments of a 10th-century Timber Arcade from Vintner's Place on the London Waterfront, *Journal of Medieval Archaeology*, 37, 79–92.

Grape, W. (1994) *The Bayeux Tapestry*. Munich: Prestel.

Griffiths, R.A. (1981) *The Reign of King Henry VI*. Berkeley: University of California Press.

Hart, C. (1999) The Bayeux Tapestry and Schools of Illumination at Canterbury. In *Anglo-Norman Studies* 22. Woodbridge: Boydell & Brewer.

Hayward Gallery Exhibition Catalogue (1984) *English Romanesque Art, 1066–1200*.

Herrick, S.K. (2007) *Imagining the Sacred Past*. Harvard: Harvard University Press.

Heslop, T.A. (2003) Orford Castle: nostalgia and sophisticated living. In R. Liddiard, *Anglo-Norman Castles*. Woodbridge: Boydell & Brewer.

Hicks, C. (2006) *The Bayeux Tapestry: The Life Story of a Masterpiece*. London: Chatto & Windus.

Higham, N.J. (1997) *The Death of Anglo-Saxon England*. Stroud: Sutton Publishing.

Higham, R. and P. Barker (1982) *Hen Domen, Montgomery: A Timber Castle on the English-Welsh Border*. London: Royal Archaeological Institute.

Higham, R. and P. Barker (1992) *Timber Castles*. Exeter: University of Exeter Press.

Hill, D. (1990) Quentovic defined. *Antiquity* 64.

Hill, D. and J. McSween (2011) The storage chest and the repairs and changes in the Bayeux Tapestry. In M.J. Lewis, G.R. Owen-Crocker and D. Terkla (eds.), *The Bayeux Tapestry: New Approaches*. Oxford: Oxbow Books.

Hoskins, W.G. (1955) *The Making of the English Landscape*, London: Hodder and Stoughton.

Hosler, J.D. (2007) *Henry II: A Medieval Soldier at War, 1147-1189*. Leiden: Brill.

Hutchinson, G. (1994) *Medieval Ships and Shipping*. Leicester: Leicester University Press.

James, T. B. (1997) *Winchester*. London: Batsford/English Heritage.

Jones, M. (1988) *Creation of Brittany*. London: Hambledon Press.

Keats-Rohan, K.S.B. (2012) Through the eye of the needle: Stigand, the Bayeux Tapestry and the beginnings of the *Historia Anglorum*. In D. Roffe (ed.), *The English and their Legacy, 900–1200*. Woodbridge: Boydell & Brewer.

Kirby, D.P. (1978) The Church in Saxon Sussex. In P. Brandon (ed.), *The South Saxons*. Chichester: Phillimore and Co. Ltd.

La Borderie, A. (1899) *Histoire de Bretagne* iii. Rennes.

Le Maho, J. (2000) La-Tour-de-Rouen, palais du duc Richard 1er (d.996). In F. Beaurepaire et J.-P. Chaline (coordination), *La Normandie vers l'an mil*. Rouen: Societé de l'Histoire de Normandie.

Legge, M.D. (1987) Bishop Odo in the Bayeux Tapestry. *Medium Aevum* 56.

Lethaby, W.R. (1906) *Westminster Abbey and the King's Craftsmen: A Study of Medieval Building*. London: Duckworth.

Lemangen, S. (2015) *La Tapisserie de Bayeux*, Bayeux: OREP edition.

Lewis, M.J. (2005) The archaeological authority of the Bayeux Tapestry. *BAR British Series* 404.

Lewis, M.J. (2007) Identity and status in the Bayeux Tapestry. In *Anglo-Norman Studies* 29. Woodbridge: Boydell & Brewer.

Lewis M.J. (2008) *The Real World of the Bayeux Tapestry*. Stroud: The History Press.

MacDougal, P. (2009) Bosham: A key Anglo-Saxon harbour. *Sussex Archaeological Collections* 147.

Marvin, W.P. (2006) *Hunting Law and Ritual in Medieval English Literature*. Woodbridge: Boydell & Brewer.

Mason E, (1996) *Westminster Abbey and its People*. Woodbridge: Boydell & Brewer.

McGrail, S. (1983) *Ancient Boats in North-West Europe*. London: Longman.

Morillo, S. (1994) *Warfare under the Anglo-Norman Kings, 1066–1135*. Woodbridge: Boydell & Brewer.

Musset, L. (2005) *The Bayeux Tapestry*. Woodbridge: Boydell & Brewer.

Neagley L.E. (2011) Portals of the Bayeux Tapestry. In M.J. Lewis, G.R. Owen-Crocker and D. Terkla (eds.), *The Bayeux Tapestry: New Approaches*. Oxford: Oxbow Books.

Neveux, F. (1996) *Bayeux et Lisieux: Villes Épiscopales de Normandie à la Fin du Moyen Age*. Caen: Éditions du Lys.

Oggins, R.S. (2004) *The Kings and Their Hawks: Falconry in Medieval England*. New Haven: Yale University Press.

Oksanen E. (2012) *Flanders and the Anglo-Norman World, 1066–1216*. Cambridge: Cambridge University Press.

Olsen, O. and Crumlin-Pedersen, O. (1967) The Skuldelev ships. *Acta Archaeologica* 38.

Overbey, K.E. (2009) Taking place: Reliquaries and territorial authority in the Bayeux Embroidery. In M.K. Foys, K.E. Overbey and D. Terkla (eds.), *The Bayeux Tapestry: New Interpretations*. Woodbridge: Boydell & Brewer.

Owen-Crocker, G.R. (1986) *Dress in Anglo-Saxon England*. Manchester: Manchester University Press.

Owen-Crocker, G.R. (2009) Stylistic variation and Roman influence in the Bayeux Tapestry. In *Peregrinations*. International Society for the Study of Pilgrimage Art, vol 2, Issue 3/4, Summer 2009.

Pastan, C.E. and S.D. White (2014) *The Bayeux Tapestry and its Contents: A Reassessment*. Woodbridge: Boydell & Brewer.

Pounds, N.J.G. (1994) *The Medieval Castle in England and Wales*. Cambridge: Cambridge University Press.

Rodwell, W. and Tatto-Brown, T. eds (2015) *Westminster 1. The Art, Architecture and Archaeology of the Royal Abbey*, British Archaeological Association, Conference Transactions XXXIX, Part 1.

Renoux, A. (1995) Palais épiscopaux des diocèses de Normandie du Mans et d'Angers (XIe-XIIIe siècle): état de la question. In P. Bouet et F. Neveux (eds.), *Les Évéques normands du XIe siècle*. Caen: Presses Universitaires de Caen.

Rowley, T. (1999), *The Normans*, Stroud: Tempus Publishing.

Rowley, T. (2013) *The Man Behind the Bayeux Tapestry: Odo, William the Conqueror's Half-Brother*. Stroud: The History Press.

Russo D.G. (1998) *Town Origins and Development in Early England, c.400–950 AD*. London: Greenwood Publishing Group.

Salzman, L.F. (ed.) (1953) *A History of the County of Sussex*. Victoria County History.

Schofield, J. (1993) *The Building of London*. London: British Museum Press.

Stalley, R. (1999) *Early Medieval Architecture*. Oxford: Oxford University Press.

Steane, J. (1985) *The Archaeology of Medieval England and Wales* London: Routledge.

Steane, J. (2003) *The Archaeology of the Medieval English Monarchy*. London: Routledge.

Stenton, F.M. (ed.) (1957) *The Bayeux Tapestry: A Comprehensive Survey*. London: Phaidon Press.

Stephenson, P. (2011) Where a Cleric and Aelfgyva. In M.J. Lewis, G.R. Owen-Crocker and D. Terkla (eds.), *The Bayeux Tapestry: New Approaches*. Oxford: Oxbow Books.

Stevenson, W.H. (1913) Senlac and the Malfosse. *English Historical Review* 28.

Taylor, A. (1992) Belrem. In *Anglo-Norman Studies* 14. Woodbridge Boydell & Brewer.

Thomas, C. (2002) *The Archaeology of Medieval London*. Stroud: Sutton Publishing.

Thomas, C., Cowie, R. and Sidell, J. (2006) The royal palace, abbey and town of Westminster on Thorney Island: Archaeological excavations (1991-8) for the London Underground Limited Jubilee Line extension project. *Museum of London Archaeology Service*, Monograph Series 22.

Thomas, G. (2010) The later Anglo-Saxon settlement at Bishopstone. *CBA*.

Thomas, G. and Knox, A. (2012) *Lyminge Excavations 2012*. Canterbury Archaeological Trust.

Turner, R. and Johnson, A. (eds) (2006) *Chepstow Castle. Its History and Buildings* Logaston: Logaston Press.

van Houts, E.M.C. (1988) The ship list of William the Conqueror. In *Anglo-Norman Studies* X. Woodbridge: Boydell & Brewer.

van Houts, E.M.C. (ed. and tr.) (1995) *The Gesta Normannorum Ducum of William of Jumièges, Orderic Vitalis and Robert of Torigni*. Oxford: Clarendon Press.

Wessex Archaeology, A259 Bexhill and Hastings Western and A259 Hastings Eastern Bypass: Evaluation Report, WA 39211c. 1996

Williams, A. (2008) *The World Before Domesday: The English Aristocracy 900–1066*. London: Continuum.

Wilson, D. (1985) *The Bayeux Tapestry*. London: Thames and Hudson.

Woodman, F. (2015), 'Edward the Confessor's Church at Westminster: An Alternative View', in Rodwell *et al* 2015, 61–68.

www.alderneybayeuxtapestry.com, accessed 25 Aug 2014

www.channel4.com/programmes/time-team-specials/4od, accessed 15 Jan 2015

www.culture24.org.uk/history-and-heritage/archaeology/art22753, accessed 30 Aug 2013.

www.learn.columbia.edu/treasuresofheaven/relics/reliquary.php, accessed 1 Feb 2016

www.mondes-normands.caen.fr/patrimoine_architectural/normand/Bonneville/index.htm, accessed 27 Aug 2013.

www.ot-montsaintmichel.com, accessed 1 Feb 2016.

Index